fractured eye

CREATION CINEMA STUDIES
CREATION PUBLISHING

fractured eye

A Journal Of Subversive Film Arts, Volume One

Edited by Stephen Barber and Jack Hunter
Published 2012 by Creation Books
ISBN 978-1-84068-189-5

fractured eye

A JOURNAL OF SUBVERSIVE FILM ARTS

1

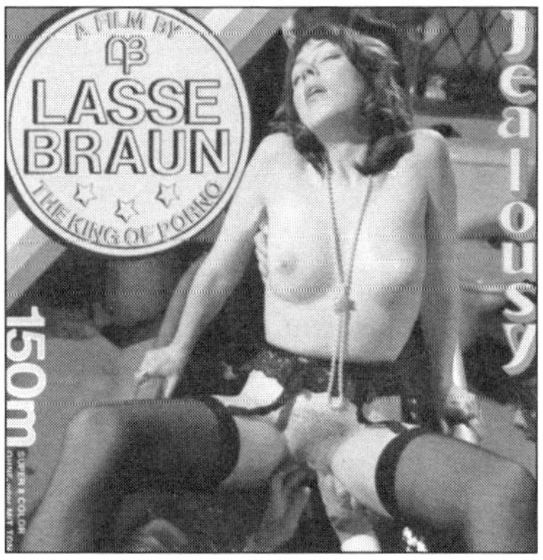

"satin party": a loop by lasse braun

Lasse Braun inaugurated his cinema of subversion in 1967 with a single aim – to smash censorship by legitimizing visual pornography, and producing it at an unprecedented artistic and commercial level. Ten years, dozens of pornographic loops and magazines, several pornographic features, and millions of dollars later, Braun arrived in London in 1977 to film a new series of short movies. This was underground film-making in a very deliberate sense; producing hardcore pornography was highly illegal in the UK and each day of covert shooting was overshadowed by the spectre of sudden arrest, imprisonment or deportation. But luckily for Lasse, the police were more intent on arresting another group of dangerous subversives, known as The Sex Pistols; while they absurdly wasted their time and tax-payers' money chasing down cruise-boats on the Thames, Braun and his crew carried on unhindered in Notting Hill and Kensington, eventually completing a twelve-loop set comprising the following titles: **Country Life**, **Jealousy**, **English Schoolgirl**, **Locked Out**, **Nazi Games**, **Satin Party**, **Tit Friction**, **Lotus Flower**, **Uncle Roger**, **Meter Maid**, **Call Girls**, and **Metamorphosis**.

Satin Party (serial number L-72) is of particular interest as it features the participation of Cosey Fanni Tutti, a stripper/dancer, porn actress, and performance artist with Coum Transmissions, a group which was at that time morphing into industrial noise pioneers Throbbing Gristle. Cosey's other porno appearances include **Sexangle**, a loop directed by John Lindsay, and **Teenage Sin**, part of the 8mm Impact XX Home Movies series. Running at around 24 minutes, **Satin Party** is among the longest loops in the "London" series, and it was also the last to be shot. To celebrate a month of successful filming, Lasse Braun decided to stage and film an orgy in an opulent Notting Hill Gate townhouse (an echo of Donald Cammell's **Performance**, made some nine years previously, which also produced pornographic footage shot on-set by Anita Pallenberg). The loop ends with a police raid, a sardonic simulation of the real raid they had all feared, but which never came.

Satin Party commences with an exterior shot of three well-dressed women arriving at the house, after which they join the party which is already underway behind its doors. Braun's first signature shot shows us a man fingering a girl's vagina as she dances, the camera staring up between her legs from floor level. The first full sex scene takes place on a couch where a naked Cosey and another female perform a double blow-job on a

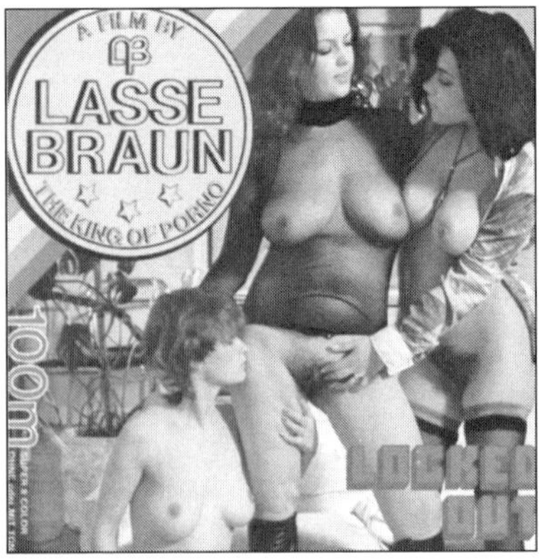

male orgiast. [This scene was also edited into a short loop entitled **Anal Sensuality**, which shows an image of Cosey on its box cover.] Braun next intercuts two sex sequences: a man fucking a Chinese girl, and a transsexual engaging with a black man. The film features a continual orgy background, as various couples can be seen fucking. The two other main sex scenes are a three-way sequence with a man and two girls, and another sequence with Cosey engaged in lesbian oral action with a red-haired girl. [This scene was also edited into a short loop entitled **Nurse Attraction**, which shows an image of Cosey on its box cover.] All the scenes are filmed with Braun's custom compositional invention and eye for the bizarre. **Satin Party** closes on a downbeat note as police officers storm the house, hauling away various participants (some naked or in mid-fuck) who are then driven off to prison in a van, reminding us of the sorry state of sexual repression in England.

Satin Party was later included (in an edited form) in the Lasse Braun loop anthology feature **Sin Dreamer**, which also contains versions or segments of the London loops **Uncle Roger**, **Country Life**, **Jealousy**, **Nazi Games**, **Call Girls**, and **Metamorphosis**. A companion feature, **Sex Maniacs**, includes parts of **English Schoolgirl**, **Tit Friction**, **Jealousy**, **Locked Out**, and **Meter Maid**. Both features were created by producer Mike Hunter (aka Gerd Wasmund), who also shot additional linking footage for both movies.

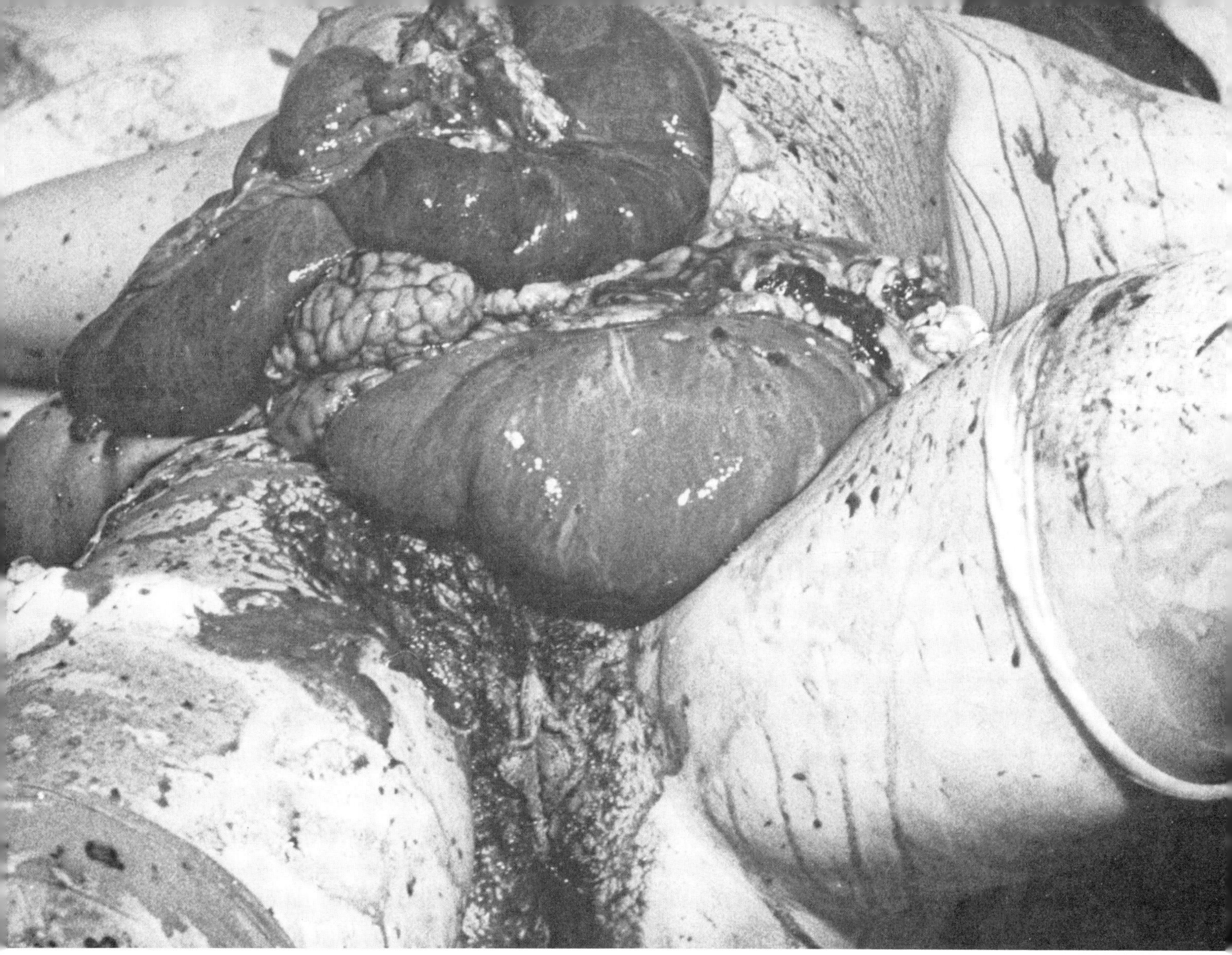

hermann nitsch: "maria conception aktion"

Maria Conception Aktion (aka **Maria-Empfängnis-Aktion-Hermann-Nitsch** aka **7.abreaktionsspiel** aka **Aktion 32**; Irm & Ed Sommer, 1970: Germany) is a 7-minute film of a performance *aktion* by Hermann Nitsch in Munich, December 1969. Out of all the four main Vienna Aktionists, Nitsch was perhaps the least filmed except for Rudolf Schwarzkogler (only one of whose aktions is known to have been captured by movie camera[1]), but **Maria Conception Aktion** makes up for that in one fell swoop. Aided and abetted by the voluptuous Hanel Koeck (muse of fetish artist Pierre Molinier) and Heinz Cibulka, Nitsch unleashes a primordial, blasphemous orgy of blood, viscera, meat and sexual pandemonium that has rarely, if ever, been equalled in cinema. Filmed in Munich, **Maria Conception Aktion** starts with bandaged figures drinking animal blood, then Koeck, dressed only in bra, panties and stockings/suspenders, being tied to a cross in a mock crucifixion; piles of animal guts are then heaped on her belly and groin, panties cut away, she starts to masturbate with the guts; meanwhile Nitsch carves an artificial vagina into a hanging lamb carcass, pulls out the viscera, covered in blood, sculpting with entrails, pouring buckets of blood over everything; prone figures are heaped with more offal, Nitsch writhes in

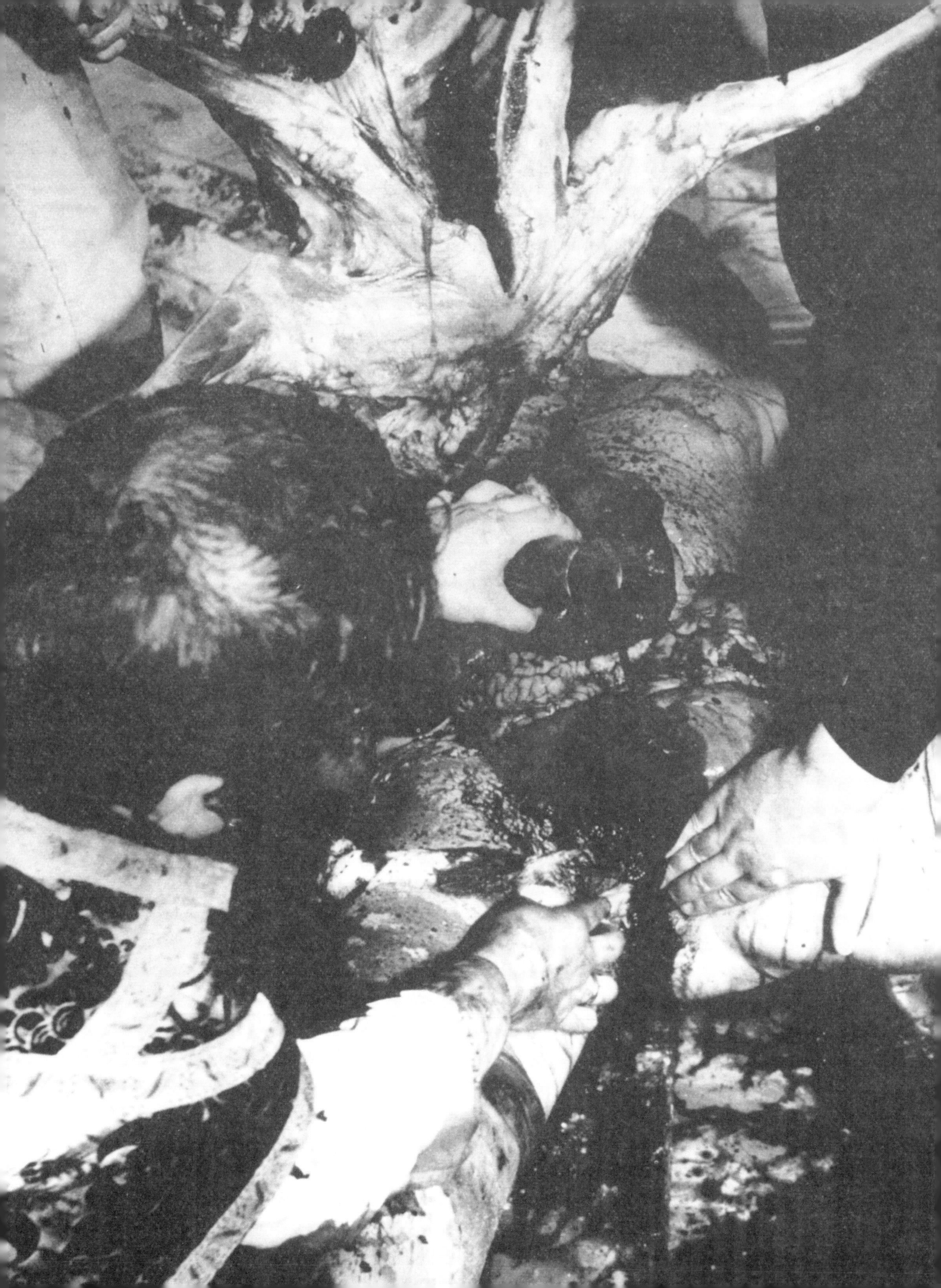

it as more carcasses are strewn about; now Koeck's thighs are spread apart on the cross, showing her open cunt, more guts and blood are poured over it, her cunt-lips being pulled apart reflecting the rending of the carcasses; she drinks and spits animal blood; Nitsch cleans out her gaping cunt, pours more blood over it, then savagely fucks her with a strap-on dildo while his acolytes douse him in blood; finally Koeck is cut down, she and the others writhe on the floor in a frenzy of carcasses, guts and blood, Nitsch finally dives between her legs, devouring her cunt as she wraps entrails around his head, before the orgiasts fall away, one by one, in blood-drenched exhaustion.

Maria-Conception-Aktion is a startling and graphic example of Nitsch's Orgies and Mysteries Theatre, the blasphemous spectacle of bloodshed, cathartic slaughter and ecstasy which he first conceived in the 1950s and which would constitute his life's work. He finally achieved the ultimate expression of this primordial rite in 1998, with a triumphant performance (filmed in digital video) of bloodshed, screaming, sensory excess and intoxication, running without cessation for six days and nights and involving several hundred revellers. Other filmed *aktions* by Nitsch include **Painting Aktion** (1962), **Aktion 13** (1965), **Aktion 15** (1965), **Aktion 18** (1966), and **Aktion 24** (1967). The directors of **Maria-Conception-Aktion**, Ed and Irm Sommer, were experimental film-makers who turned to making erotic 16mm shorts at the end of the 60s; their other films include **Striptease And Emancipation** (1969), **Contact** (1970) and **Lovely Love** (1971). Hanel Koeck also appeared in several *aktion* films by Otto Muehl, including the infamous **Shit-Bastard** (1969).

Notes

1. **Schwarzkogler 18.12.65** is a film of the artist's 4th *aktion*, shot by Günter Brus.

into the zone: pierre guyotat and film

Pierre Guyotat's work has an intricate rapport with cinema, from its origins: an intensive, sensorial, experiential rapport. Guyotat's work, in many ways, is an experience of cinema – the space of cinema, the history of cinema, and the history that exists around and in tension with cinema – that infiltrates both that work and also his corporeal presence in relation to the film image. Guyotat has also made a number of films, notably in the course of his journeys of the 1960s and 70s, and at moments of transition and transit in his work. His links with cinema are profound ones, and the power of images – together with the power of the experience of cinematic space – often inflects his work's trajectory. The preoccupation with cinema is a 'lived' one for Guyotat: an inhabitation of images of cinema and the history that is instilled in cinema, together with the gestures and faces and traces of cities shown in films. At the same time, that preoccupation with film also forms a perpetual transformation from image to language, and from language back to the film image. Since the 1960s, Guyotat has been concerned incessantly with the question of accomplishing impossibilities in language, and it has been cinema – with its impossible images, time and space, and movements – that has often irresistibly presented a model, or a set of revelations, to him, for his work, whether he wanted that model or not.

The first filmic site for Guyotat, in the 1940s, was the cinema in his home village, the 'Foyer' cinema, whose name indicates the intimacy mediated by cinemas of that era, especially in the context of life in the mountainous regions of southern France where images appeared primarily through the medium either of photography or film. Many of the images which marked Guyotat most deeply in the late 1940s postwar period were photographic images of concentration camps and lines of refugees crossing destroyed European wastelands; photography possessed its own time, while film images – especially in newsreels – went too fast for perception, mixing everything at full speed, during an era when it was essential to examine all images for the duration they deserved, since they held otherwise unseizable, unbearable history. By contrast, film directly incited sensations, and those sensations then multiplied themselves to infinity. Guyotat remembered that: 'As a child, in the newsreels, a boxing match between women violently stirred me.' His book *Coma* also contains a memory from his time watching films in the Foyer cinema: a memory from 1947, when he was seven years old, of a film without a title, partially re-imagined in his account (but recognisable as John Huston's film of that year, **Let There Be Light**), about traumatised prisoners of war. Guyotat evokes the return to life of a totally amnesiac soldier who is corporeally seized by that furious moment of reactivation, which operates simultaneously through memory and the body.

The Cinémathèque Française in Paris was the seminal filmic site for Guyotat's experience of the city, in the early 1960s, following his return from the Algerian War. In his notebooks from November 1962, when he was about to arrive in Paris from Algeria, he imagines that arrival as an inhabitation of the Cinémathèque, where he would soon be watching three screenings each day (as many cinema-crazed people of his age did, in that era), joyfully obsessed by film, constantly reading books of film history, and seeing celebrated directors introducing their films there; for Guyotat's memory of the time, the most important of those near-magical contacts were his sightings of Dreyer and Chaplin.

Buñuel's film **Los Olvidados** was a crucial inspiration for Guyotat's first major novel, *Tomb for 500,000 Soldiers*. That caustic, hallucinatory film, dissecting conflicts between young inhabitants of Mexico City's peripheral zones, formed one of the vital sources of the novel. In a newspaper interview from the beginning of 1965, Guyotat asserted that the idea for the novel had come to him after repeated viewings of the film. The book's origins are

impossible to reduce to only one source, and form a vast, multiple archive of images and texts, but at the time of the novel's writing, Guyotat was actively searching out films which would provide examples of combinations and editing techniques which he could apply to his sequences of all-engulfing combat and massacre in the novel. In his notebooks of the era, the English word 'like' often appears, designating a rapport of parallel conception which linked his creative process to films such as Eisenstein's **Alexander Nevsky**; in those films, spectacular battles always transmutated into catastrophes. He also searched films for the presences of noise: the sounds of fires, and the cries of animals distinctly heard even within filmic sequences of battles and massacres. At the time when he was writing *Tomb For 500,000 Soldiers*, Guyotat also watched more austere and mysterious films, in order to refine a transparent form of language within which to insert a dark content, often transected with delirium, and articulated through repetition. That form of language would be one intimately close to film, and capable of containing contrary and irreconcilable elements, to project them towards his reader. In his notebooks, he wrote: 'Take the example of **The Eclipse** by Antonioni for the taking-forward of a number of scenes. Scenes that will be naked, that will exact delirium, dramatically. That will give delirium an order and a necessity.' Films also accompanied Guyotat in his engagement of the 1960s with the question of how to end a text or novel: a pressing question, in the context of a body of work in which almost nothing can ever end, and in which the movement of narration is almost always torn out of its ostensible moment of finishing, and propelled towards infinity. In the work of the Czech filmmaker, Jan Němec, Guyotat saw examples in which a film's deep layering of time and memory could explode, as he wrote, 'on the ending with the final image'.

After that intensive engagement with film during the writing of *Tomb For 500,000 Soldiers*, Guyotat's rapport with film (as well as with other art forms) changed. It became rarer, more accidental, but also more concentrated, as well as being surrounded by his social engagements of the end of the 1960s, and their aftermath. That rapport continued throughout the period of journeys which led to Guyotat's state of coma in 1981. For Guyotat, a pivotal topographical and corporeal correspondence with cinema's history was that the clinic in which he was treated in the months following that coma – the Clinique Jeanne d'Arc in the Parisian suburb of Saint-Mandé – was the same clinic in which Dreyer had convalesced in the 1920s following the exhausting film-shoot for **The Passion Of Joan Of Arc** in Paris: a film very closely tied, in many ways, with Guyotat's book *Coma*.

In *Coma*, Guyotat recounts his experience, in July 1981, several months before his fall into a state of coma, of joining a group of friends in the town of Montauban to watch the film **The Clash Of The Titans** (an

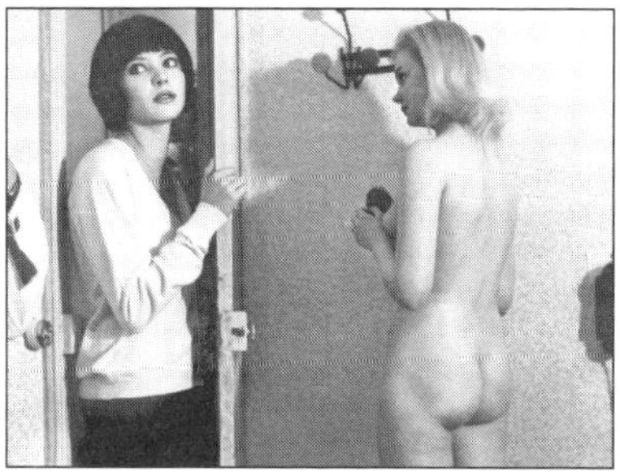

English film based on Greek mythology). Guyotat's separation from the rest of the cinema audience is total and determining. He writes: 'This film which made its spectators roar with ironic laughter: I entered into it as though into my future coma.' The experience of a film – in extreme solitude – can be so strong and engulfing that it accords with the experience of a coma. And the screen on which the film is projected forms the aperture which offers liberation, or leads directly into death. Guyotat describes the figure in the film of Andromeda, who is split in two, against her will, existing simultaneously in the world and in death. In *Coma*, her figure is no longer that of Andromeda, but instead that of a creature who has been reinvented, half-human, half-goddess, and engaged in an act of tightrope-walking, between the corporeal and the void. But the cinematic space also possesses its corporeal presence in *Coma*, and during the film's screening, Guyotat descends a set of stairs beneath the auditorium, to vomit his pills in the toilets, but continues to hear, from that infernal subterranea of the cinema, the overhead voices of the gods battling over his future.

In the context of a reading and exhibition of his work in Marseilles, Guyotat compiled a list of the films which had been most important for his work and life, including Japanese films by Kurosawa and Ozu, a film by Léos Carax, and Godard's 1962 film, **Vivre Sa Vie**. And it was Godard, almost forty years after **Vivre Sa Vie**, who incorporated Guyotat's voice into his film **The Origin Of The Twenty-First Century**, commissioned for the Cannes Film Festival of 2000. Guyotat's voice appears in the film with an almost visual and corporeal presence, in fragments and bursts: a voice which becomes a tangible layer of sound, above the layer of Godard's film-images, entirely taken from archives and newsreels, and showing, in part, the massacres and revolutionary acts of the twentieth century, alongside extracts, each of several seconds, from fiction films, including **Los Olvidados**. That strange amalgam, of images of massacres and filmic nostalgia, appears necessary in order to mark, in a permanent way, the existence of film as a medium of history, violence and imagination, before film's total abandonment and vanishing, in the digital era. Guyotat's vocal reading, from his book *Progenitors*, also forms an incantation about images, and at the heart of images – and recalls his stated desire, at the time in the late 1960s of his writing of his novel *Eden, Eden, Eden* and his alliance with the journal 'Tel Quel', to make his texts actively create and generate images, as an act directed against abstraction. In **The Origin Of The Twenty-First Century**, Godard often stalls his film's movement, in order simply to show dates: the key dates of the twentieth century, and simultaneously, the dates of an individual history. Among those dates are 1940, that of the Fall of France to the German army, and also the year of Guyotat's birth; 1960, the year of Guyotat's attachment to the

films of Bergman and Bresson (especially **Pickpocket**), and of his decision to leave France for the war in Algeria; and 1975, the year of the publication of Guyotat's novel *Prostitution* and of the murder of a close friend in Marseilles. Even against its will, the filmic image cannot prevent itself from telling multiple histories.

After their collaboration on **The Origin Of The Twenty-First Century**, a period of discussion between Godard and Guyotat followed on the possibility of making a jointly conceived film; the project was abandoned. Alongside his contacts with Godard, other intersections – often brief, but intensive – with directors and actors have marked Guyotat's work, notably that with Lillian Gish, from whom Guyotat receives an affectionate kiss in his book *Coma* (whose filmic and photographic illustrations finish with a still of Gish in the film **The Wind**). Guyotat also had encounters with producers seeking to film his books, including a calamitous meeting with Claude Nedjar whose memory proved so unbearable to Guyotat that, in *Coma*, it is transposed into an encounter with the artist Michel Nedjar.

The films which Guyotat has made himself began at the moment when he arrived in Paris for the first time, at the age of nineteen, in 1959 – three years before his second arrival in Paris following his time in Algeria. That process of filmmaking was conceived by Guyotat as a means to research and visually seize gestures and acts, and to make spaces and objects materialise. They were films with their own existence and autonomy, but at the same time formed an element in the assembly of his texts and novels. In *Coma*, Guyotat evokes his filming in the Parc Saint-Cloud, to the west of Paris: 'I film statues, flora, animals, insects, birds, I wait for long periods of time, at the far side of the park from its entrance, beside burrows and holes, for the emergence of the rabbit, the mole, the snake, I wait.' During his two journeys through postwar Algeria, each of several months, in early 1967 and early 1968, Guyotat filmed mountains and villagers. In his notebooks, he used an English word for those films: his 'rushes', as though that word aimed to capture, with rapidity, and even after a long wait, the gestures and landscapes he was looking for, just as he had previously aimed to seize, in film, the animals of the Parc Saint-Cloud. While writing *Eden, Eden, Eden*, in December 1968, in his apartment in the Parisian suburb of Vitry-sur-Seine, he projected those films of Algeria for himself, in order to activate and sustain his writing process, and to infiltrate it with film-images; those 'rushes' contained images of flowers and animals, but also, as he noted, that of 'a lorry-driver, jeans covered in semen'. In 1998, while Guyotat was preparing *Progenitors*, I sometimes accompanied him to cafes in the Belleville district, in which he filmed, with a hidden video-camera, transactions and chance gestures. All of Guyotat's own films, over a period of five decades, form a layer of images which, in

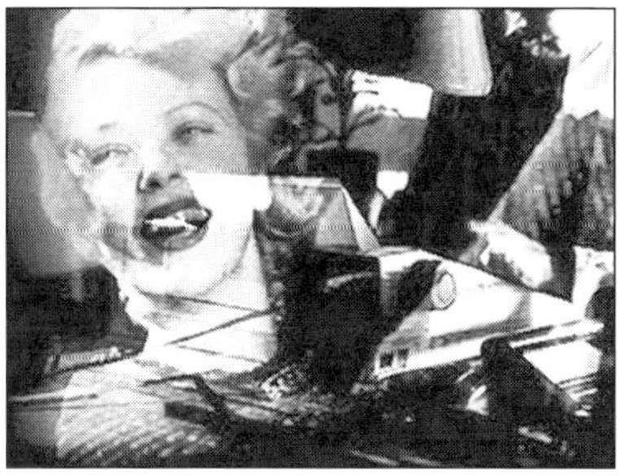  

its rapport with his texts, resonates with his voice's presence in Godard's **The Origin Of The Twenty-First Century**. Guyotat's own films constitute an intermittent presence, above his texts: film as an unforeseen and volatile illumination, in the form of fragments.

I visited the spaces of cinemas with Guyotat on two occasions. The first was in July 1991, at the site of the concentration camp, Sachsenhausen, to the north of Berlin, where his uncle, Hubert Vianney, had been killed in 1943 after being deported for resistance activities from France. During the recently-vanished era of the East German state, one of the camp's wooden barracks had been adapted into a cinema space, where a single, twenty-minute film, the celluloid worn-out and the Russian-language soundtrack disintegrating into cacophony, was projected repeatedly. The film showed the camp's liberation by the Soviet army in 1945. Even in summer, the concentration-camp cinema was frozen, and empty, with only Guyotat and I, and the decrepit old projectionist, positioned menacingly behind us, at the back of the room. With extreme concentration, Guyotat entered into the images and the sounds of the film. Afterwards, there was a jarringly immediate transition, from the film images in darkness, to the execution terrains and experimentation blocks of the camp outside. The film image, with its unique space and time, can launch such moments of outlandish transition – that can never be repeated, that can not even be lived, except in the form of a text. Shortly afterwards, the camp's topography abruptly changed, and the cinema-barracks was demolished. The second visit to a cinema space with Guyotat, around seven years later, was in Paris, at the Forum des Images. We were watching a film Guyotat was deeply attached to: Georges Lacombe's **The Zone**, from 1928, shot on the impoverished peripheries of Paris, and showing the faces and gestures of that wasteland's inhabitants, especially those of children. During the screening, Guyotat kept up a whispered vocal commentary on the film's images, as though his voice were that of the figure in silent Japanese cinema – the 'benshi' – who stood beside the screen and deployed his voice to accentuate and isolate those special elements of the images that it was vital to keep in memory, and never consign to oblivion: those elements that would irresistibly come to possess another existence, in a space beyond that of cinema.

the skladanowsky brothers: the devil knows

Introduction

In exploring the final detritus of cinematic projection, embodied in the shattered and gutted projection-boxes, the dust-encrusted cans of negated celluloid, and the once-luxurious, now-decrepit auditoria of the cinema-palaces of the 1920s, whose façades still constellate the Broadway avenue, in Los Angeles' Downtown, for my book *Abandoned Images*, I often experienced the sense that filmic time was held on a knife-edge in that precarious urban location, erasing any linearity of futures or pasts or presents, and could veer from one extreme to another, from film's end to its origins, or back again, in the blink of an iris. And that preoccupation with the seminal welding-together of cinematic projection's end and its initiation then took me from Los Angeles to Berlin, where two near-forgotten brothers, Max and Emil Skladanowsky, had originated public film-projection by showing a programme of their own films, on celluloid stock, to a paying audience at the Wintergarten Ballroom, in Berlin's Central Hotel, on 1 November 1895, almost two months before the Lumière Brothers undertook their own first film-projection for a public audience, at the Grand Café in Paris, on 28 December of that year. The Skladanowsky Brothers were almost immediately overtaken, in both technological and aesthetic domains, by their many rivals, so that they became stranded in film-historical no-man's-land, their status overlayered within the conflicting, multiplicitous traces both of film's origins and of the onset of film-projection. Just as the end-point of film is vitally indeterminate, but can be tentatively excavated in fragments in the lavish ruins of cinema-palaces, the origin of film is itself correspondingly indeterminable: quantifiable only within limits, in terms of speed, media, audience and location, among other factors, and also in the non-collaborative, often-vitriolic competitiveness of film's 1890s pioneers. The impasses generated by such multiple and irreconcilable narratives invariably lead to re-invention, in which the time of film's origin becomes malleable, subject to contrary imperatives according to the priorities and demands of narration, with the result that any origin forms a tenuous one, in its telling. The Wintergarten film-screening of 1895 constitutes an initiating event that is tightly enmeshed within conflicting historical, film-historical, urban-historical and cultural strata, and subject, across the intervening decades, to an intermittent process of visibility, oscillating between prominence and near-extinguishment. But the Skladanowsky Brothers' hold on the temporal origin of film-projection remains a distinctive and ineradicable one, in many ways perversely enhanced by the vanishing of many of its traces and locations, within the urban space of Berlin.

The Skladanowsky Brothers hand-constructed their own projector, with the explicit aim of enabling spectators to assemble in a specific location, orient their vision towards a large-scale screen, and view a programme of films, together, as an audience. They named their projector the 'Bioskop', from the Greek: 'to see life': an instrument that would exact an ocular and sensorial form of entrancement. They also built their own film camera and shot a number of films, and had already reached the stage of experimenting with test-projections of those films, for private audiences of friends and colleagues, in the entertainment room of a cafe in one of the industrial districts of northern Berlin, before they were commissioned by the directors of a far larger and prestigious venue, the Wintergarten Ballroom, to project those films to a paying public, over the duration of a month, as part of a programme that would predominantly feature live performances. After undertaking those projections, they toured across northern Europe with their films, for a period of eighteen months, before abruptly encountering obstacles which halted their experiments and consigned them to oblivion for several decades. The two brothers, Max and Emil, possessed elements both of showmen and of untrained, resourceful inventors, though Max worked principally with the technical aspects of their filmmaking and projection, and Emil's primary contribution involved the promotion of their inventions and arrangements for bringing those inventions to public audiences.

The audiences for public manifestations of moving images, across the pre-filmic and early-cinema eras, from the 1880s to the beginning of the twentieth century, ranged widely. Eadweard Muybridge's scrapbooks of annotated press-articles on his pre-filmic public slide-projections of moving-images, with his 'Zoopraxiscope' device, indicate a breadth of spectators encompassing artists and scientists, aristocrats and royalty, alongside the public audiences that attended his lecture-demonstrations at the Chicago World's Fair in 1893. From 1905, the audiences and venues for film-projection began to acquire elements of a disreputable aura, through the prevalence of nickelodeons, their projection-spaces often improvised through the adaptation of shopfront rooms in rundown urban areas, intimately packed with spectators. The envisaging of a moving-image audience, and of film-spectatorship itself, constituted an intensively mutable one, in perpetual transformation and reorientation, across those formative decades. But the public audience for the Skladanowsky Brothers' first film-projection event, on 1 November 1895, had a particular form: it was a wealthy audience, of sensation-avid Berliners and international travellers, in sharp distinction to the relatively impoverished artisan-showmen who projected their films to that audience.

The Skladanowsky Brothers possessed a specific urban location, in their attachment to industrial northern Berlin, especially the heavily-populated tenement-districts of Prenzlauerberg and Pankow, which were inhabited at that time mainly by factory-workers, employed notably in the area's many breweries; as well as living in those districts, Max and Emil Skladanowsky also rented their workshops there, and shot their first film on the rooftop of a building above one of the area's main avenues, the Schönhauser Allee, its images holding a panorama of factory-chimneys and church-steeples. When the brothers made incursions into central Berlin, and took on engagements to demonstrate their inventions in deluxe venues, such as the Wintergarten Ballroom, it was largely unfamiliar territory for them. But alongside their localised urban attachments, they were also itinerant showmen, who had already spent many years crisscrossing Europe for performances of their earlier inventions and spectacles. That quality of itinerancy, with its incessant exploratory trajectories, is imprinted too in the work of many other critical figures of the first decades of moving-images: Muybridge, above all, with his travels from Kingston-upon-Thames to San Francisco and out into the then-remote regions of California, such as Yosemite Valley, and also Louis Le Prince, who shot the first-ever film, in 1888, while displaced from France to the industrial English city of Leeds, before mysteriously disappearing without trace in the course of his travels. The Skladanowsky Brothers' work took place in fixed, localised parameters in northern Berlin, while simultaneously being encompassed by spatial dimensions that rapidly expanded through the necessity of making public that work.

In many ways, it is the volatile city of Berlin itself which makes the Skladanowsky Brothers' projection-event insurge into life, as though the localised, internally-focused dimension of their work, devised on the urban periphery, were being overruled through the all-engulfing compulsion to strip innovations down and thereby extract new sensations for the constant revivification of the city-centre's lucrative public spectacles. In the 1890s, after many decades of being dismissed as a militaristic, austere city, Berlin had finally emerged as a pre-eminent European site of avid, visually-based spectatorship and lavish over-consumption, manifested above all in the form of variety reviews, staged in luxurious venues such as the Wintergarten Ballroom. The urban historian Alexandra Richie notes: 'The new reviews extolled the virtues of the big city, glorying in its consumerism and cosmopolitan nature and advertising new forms of entertainment which would later be associated exclusively with the Weimar period.'(1) It was in that context that the Skladanowsky Brothers' film-projection event took place: swallowed-alive by that desire for urban spectacle, but simultaneously, in some ways, a profoundly misplaced, aberrant presence within it, as though, even at its origin, film possessed an element of the resistant inassimilability and idiosyncrasy that formed such an essential part of its future history.

The Skladanowsky Brothers

In many ways, the Skladanowsky Brothers conjured public film-projection into existence, their blind determination indicating that they were aware of undertaking something unprecedented and original, and at the same time, unsure exactly what direction they were heading in, or precisely how to accomplish their plans, technologically or financially, but, out of audacity, simply heading on (like the young bell-founder in the final sequence of Tarkovsky's film **Andrei Rublev**). Like that of Muybridge, the Skladanowsky Brothers' work forms a volatile amalgam of showmanship and invention, with, in their case, the former element often taking the upper hand. In the way in which their career shifted abruptly and illogically, intersecting directly with film for a relatively short period, and also in their capacity to vanish almost without trace and reappear unexpectedly, decades later, in a different guise, they are, in one sense, immediacy-obsessed 'tricksters'. The press reviews of their Wintergarten Ballroom projection-event intimate something of the near-diabolical transmutations which the unleashing of film-images into the audience's space generated; although enthralled, those spectators appeared simultaneously disturbed, as though subject to a maleficent, askew conjuring-trick able to steal-away their faculties, their hold upon time and reality, and even their corporeal presence. But alongside that capacity to initiate the uncanny, capricious power of film-projection, with its uniquely mysterious aura, the Skladanowsky Brothers were also irrepressible, keenly-focused inventors, finetuned by their social and urban origins to disregard all setbacks and calamities.

The Skladanowsky Brothers, like much of the population of industrial northern Berlin, originated from a social history of displacement, with their name revealing Polish family origins, their ancestors having relocated to the city in the early nineteenth century at a time of mass migration from the impoverished rural regions to the east of Berlin.(2) After the Nazis took power in 1933, their main priority, in assessing the potential for the Skladanowskys' innovations in film to be co-opted into their nationalistic and expulsive agenda, was to determine whether the brothers came from a family of Polish Jews. Their father was a skilled glass-worker but also a performative showman, involved with developing popular public spectacles using 'Nebelbilder': literally, 'fog-pictures': a particular variant of magic-lantern projections that often exhibited terrifying or macabre images; however, the Skladanowsky family's adaptation of 'Nebelbilder' spectacles focused particularly on historical and mythical scenes, and on spectacular landscapes. Their involvement in 'Nebelbilder' spectacles was situated during the medium's last phase; its main decades of popularity were from the 1800s to the 1890s. Sequences of non-photographic glass slides, hand-painted or inscribed with images, were projected in intricate, rapid sequences, onto a large screen, with complex dissolves and overlayered optical effects, sound-elements, and an ongoing vocal narration. Although he had received only a limited apprenticeship in glass-making, Max Skladanowsky was especially proficient in constructing multi-lens 'Nebelbilder' devices, capable of simultaneously projecting up to eight or nine separate sequences of images. The two brothers, Max and Emil, accompanied their father on numerous cross-European tours of 'Nebelbilder' spectacles in the years from 1879 until 1895, from their mid-teens to early thirties; their older brother, Eugen, worked for several decades as a clown and acrobat, employed by prominent European circuses for touring engagements, and was not closely involved in their experiments with film-projection. The Skladanowsky Brothers' final 'Nebelbilder' tours of the mid-1890s were undertaken without their father; they re-named themselves 'The Hamilton Brothers', and began to experiment with incorporating new elements, such as fireworks displays and water-spectacles, into their performances, in order to accentuate an atmosphere of innovation.

In part, that obsession with expansion and innovation, and their capacity to design and execute intricate projection devices, led the Skladanowsky Brothers to film. Although the first films had been shot several years previously, in 1888, by the engineer and inventor Louis Le Prince, the technological capacity to project films before public audiences had not been realized in the intervening years; many inventors, including Edison, saw the development of public film-projection as a dead-end, and potentially worthless, while other inventors from engineering backgrounds, including Le Prince himself, approached the dilemmas surrounding film-projection with conflicting imperatives and aims from those of the Skladanowsky Brothers. In some ways, after the demands of his excessive, multiple-projection 'Nebelbilder' devices, the realization of Max Skladanowsky's film-projector, the 'Bioskop', may have been in some ways a less exacting challenge: almost an exercise in streamlining his previous work. The Lumière Brothers, in Lyons, operated on a sophisticated and well-funded technological basis, in contrast to the Skladanowsky Brothers' artisanal and impecunious form of production in Berlin; but, as with the Lumière Brothers, Max Skladanowsky flexibly meshed precedents and pre-existing experiments. Such technologies were, to varying extents, accessible for adaptation, through accounts in patents and trade journals, and could, for itinerant performers such as the Skladanowsky Brothers, often be witnessed at close proximity during the course of their travels around Europe. At the same time, the Skladanowsky Brothers' movement into filmmaking and film-projection forms an aberration and an unprecedented leap into the dark, exhibiting a reckless desire for innovation akin to that of Muybridge, with their conception, however partial, of film as possessing a distinctive entity as a new moving-image medium, with, integral to that medium, the amassing in front of a projection-screen of an admission-paying audience.

The Skladanowsky Brothers devoted their primary attention to the medium of film from 1894, during breaks between their 'Nebelbilder' tours. Although Max Skladanowsky retrospectively backdated the construction of his first film camera, and of his shooting of experimental test film-footage, to 1892, even according a specific date to that first act of filmmaking in Germany, 20 August 1892, the historian Joachim Castan has established that a far more probable date for the film-footage was that of the summer or autumn months of 1894, with the possibility that Max Skladanowsky had been gradually developing his camera, towards that eventual experiment with filmmaking, since 1892 or 1893.(3) Such strategic or hallucinatory manipulations of time were rife, among early cinema's competitive participants, in the subsequent decades' establishment of stratified chronologies and 'formative events' for film. Since the Wintergarten Ballroom film-projection event would only take place in November 1895, Max Skladanowsky justified the inexplicable three-year delay, from his own 1892 starting-date, as being the result of the consistent refusal of funds for the development of his experiments, by bank-managers who derided his plans as being mad and delusional; the financial necessity of constantly having to leave Berlin to undertake extensive 'Nebelbilder' tours had also contributed to the long delay. In 1925, he asserted: 'I could really have made the world the gift of cinema three years earlier.'(4)

The date of the Skladanowsky Brothers' first engagement with film as a medium has vanished in those retrospective conjurations of memory. But by July 1895, they definitively possessed the three vital artefacts for the exhibition of self-shot films to an audience: a film camera, films, and a film projector. As well as having assembled a programme of their own films by that time, they had also hand-constructed both their camera and projector, in their workshop, housed in a five-storey building containing innumerable other artisans' workshops, in a small street that led off the Schönhauser Allee avenue in the Prenzlauerberg district of northern Berlin. While the Skladanowsky Brothers, as adept glass-makers, had previously been able to produce all of their own, hand-painted glass-plate negatives for their 'Nebelbilder' spectacles, they had needed for the first time to order an industrially-produced medium, Eastman-Kodak celluloid film-stock, for their new experiments. But with everything in place, they now envisaged their first public film-projections.

The Wintergarten Ballroom Film-Projection

The Skladanowsky Brothers undertook their experimental film-screenings in the entertainment room of a large cafe, the Café Sello, in July 1895, projecting films which they had shot two months earlier. The Café Sello was located on the avenue which led from the Prenzlauerberg to Pankow districts of northern Berlin; it was a popular venue for factory workers to drink beer and dance to music. In the future, the entertainment room would become one of Berlin's first cinemas, before being demolished in 1927 and a new, purpose-built cinema, the Tivoli, constructed in its place; the Tivoli, situated in the postwar eastern zone of Berlin, survived the decades of East Germany intact, but not the redevelopment frenzy of the re-unified city, being demolished in 2003 and the site used for a supermarket. The Skladanowsky Brothers invited small, non-paying audiences of friends and fellow photographic artisans and showmen to their test-screenings. Emil Skladanowsky's role was to publicise the brothers' innovations, and Franz Dorn and Julius Baron, the proprietors of the far grander entertainment venue, the Wintergarten Ballroom, attended one of the experimental screenings. Dorn and Baron had taken over the Wintergarten eight years earlier and transformed it into an upmarket variety review venue, one of the most successful in Europe, in which original, international spectacles were especially prized by the audience, though the programme's format and content also drew on that of the small-scale local satirical cabaret-shows, of story-telling and music, distinctive to Berlin, that were pervasive at that time in cafes and beerhalls in industrial areas of the city, such as the Café Sello. Impressed by what they saw of the Skladanowsky Brothers' experiments, Dorn and Baron decided to commission the brothers to demonstrate their film-projector as part of the variety review spectacle they were developing for the month of November, four months into the future; a contract for the engagement was signed in September. But the Wintergarten proprietors were not only interested in the Skladanowsky Brothers' film-projection 'act' for that spectacle, and were searching for attractions in any medium that could serve to seize the attention of their innovation-avid audiences; they also engaged the brothers for the entirety of the preceding month, October, to present an entirely different attraction: a water-theatre spectacle which the brothers had recently been developing as an addition to their 'Nebelbilder' performances, in the form of a spectacular re-staging of the Roman Empire-era sea-battle of Alexandria.

Max Skladanowsky had hand-built his film-projector, the dual lens Bioskop, in his workshop, from wood, glass and steel components, during the months immediately preceding the Café Sello test-screenings. It was entirely his own work, and used a dissolve technique adapted from his previous 'Nebelbilder' projectors; he had commissioned a set of steel parts from a nearby artisans' workshop, and bought lamps for the projector's two lens, but had assembled everything singlehandedly. The result was an unprecedented, irreplicable and idiosyncratic artefact: one of its kind, as with Muybridge's Zoopraxiscope – and utterly dissimilar, in its effective but maladroit construction, from the far more technically proficient device employed by the Lumière Brothers, for their own film-projections in December of that year. The projector used a manually-turned wooden handle with a metal chain, which advanced two separate reels of film, their trajectory extending, via revolving cogs at the base of each side of the projector, almost to floor-level. To reach the projection-speed of 16 frames per second necessary for the images' movement to be perceived as a continuous sequence by the human eye, without excessive flicker, each film's images were assigned alternately to the two reels, and a serrated, revolving circular steel-plate, positioned in front of the two lens and regulated by the handle which also advanced the film-reels, allowed one lens to project while the other was obscured. Max Skladanowsky used his Bioskop projector for both the Café Sello and Wintergarten Ballroom events.

The Wintergarten Ballroom was situated within the lavish Central Hotel, one of Berlin's new, grand hotels, modelled on those of Paris and New York, and taking up an entire street-block in the Friedrichstrasse, an avenue of shopping arcades and restaurants in the centre of the city; the hotel was one of the first buildings to be seen by travellers disembarking from trains at the adjacent Friedrichstrasse railway station. The ballroom was a vast, elongated and glass-roofed space with several stages, extending from one end of the hotel to the other, along its ground floor; its clientele sat around circular tables, on several levels, rather than in rows. That clientele encompassed both wealthy, elegantly dressed Berliners, avid for new sensations, and also the hotel's international guests, who reflected Berlin's abrupt expansion as a new destination for prosperous travellers. As Alexandra Richie notes: 'a million visitors a year were arriving via the new water and rail networks which encircled the city, and the small dank inns of old gave way to the newest additions to the Berlin skyline, the grand hotels. In the late nineteenth century the size and style of hotels were considered a measure of the city's greatness, and Berliners were eager to compete with their rivals.'(5) The Wintergarten programme was not intended for spectators from the overcrowded and impoverished industrial areas of the city, nor for its artists and scientists. That site of the Skladanowsky Brothers' initiatory film-projection event would vanish almost fifty years later, when the Central Hotel was destroyed by British wartime bombing on 21 June 1944; the ballroom's roof-less ruins survived for several years before being dynamited and razed by the East German authorities in the 1950s and left as a wasteland. The site is currently occupied by newly-built multi-storey offices and shops.

The Skladanowsky Brothers' film-projection event began on 1 November and continued for four weeks, with a total of 23 projections in all. The entire evening's programme lasted for over three hours and was held daily at 7.30pm, with the Sunday shows beginning at 7pm. The Skladanowsky Brothers' contribution to the programme appeared on advertising posters mid-way down the hoardings, with an exclamatory emphasis on its status as a never previously experienced innovation. Top-billing went to Mlle Gabriele Juniori, advertised as travelling to Berlin 'from the Empire Theatre in London', along with other acts, such as Mr Tompson ('with his three elephants'), 'Die Wüstensohne' ('The Sons of the Desert'), and 'Griffin und Dubois' ('eccentrics'). The Wintergarten Ballroom held 1,500 spectators and each show was invariably at full capacity, but not all of the audience watched the Skladanowsky Brothers' films. Their contribution to the evening was spatially assigned to a small side-stage at the northern end of the auditorium, away from the main stage, and could only be experienced by spectators sitting around tables directly in front of the screen. And the film-projection was kept until the conclusion of the evening's entertainment, when part of the audience had already dispersed. The curtained screen was surrounded by elaborate gilt decorations featuring winged angels and mythical figures. The Skladanowsky Brothers' film-projections lasted for around fifteen minutes in total.(6) The screen had to be kept wet to enhance its transparence and the clarity of the film-images; rear-projection was used, with the Bioskop situated directly behind the screen, rather than in front of it, and a loud music score had been especially composed, capable of drowning out the cacophony of the projector's operation.(7)

The film-projections were successful; although the Skladanowsky Brothers had no fallback device on hand in case the Bioskop malfunctioned, the month's projections passed without major mishap. Press reviews of the

Wintergarten programme especially emphasised the three performing elephants as the evening's main attraction, but the Skladanowsky Brothers' contribution was evoked as being well-received, by audiences who responded with prolonged applause and threw flowers at the screen. Max and Emil Skladanowsky appeared on stage at the conclusion of their projections, appearing from opposite sides of the screen and thereby replicating the content of the final film in their programme, in which they had been filmed performing the same manoeuvre. Berlin newspapers of the time were rarely critical of variety reviews staged by the city's principal venues, since they depended on advertising revenue from those same venues; no criticism was made, for example, of the technical limitations of the Skladanowsky Brothers' projections, which were praised for being innovative and enthralling, but with a distinct undertone of unease. The Berlin newspaper, the *Staatsburger Zeitung*, reviewed the projections on 5 November 1895: 'The skilful technician employs delightful moments of photography here, bringing them in enlarged form into representation, but in a living rather than stilted form. How he does it, only the devil knows.'(8) In that evocation of the devil omnisciently masterminding the Skladanowsky Brothers' film-projections, a trace is present of the future suspicions of outlandishness and ungodliness, closely associated with film and its cinematic sites for their first thirty or so years, before such qualms were finally dispelled in the 1920s by the architectural lavishness of 'cathedrals' or 'palaces' of film, their decor often literally replicating that of religious buildings, such as Segovia Cathedral, and embodied above all in that era's designs for the cinemas of Los Angeles' Broadway district.

The Skladanowsky Brothers had been paid a substantial sum – 2,500 gold marks – by the Wintergarten Ballroom's proprietors for the month of November 1895.(9) The success of their projections, at such a prominent venue, led to further commissions, but they had only achieved the first public film-projection event by a hairsbreadth, and that success rapidly unravelled. The brothers were contracted for an engagement at the prestigious Folies Bergère venue in Paris, to begin on 1 January 1896, and travelled to Paris with the Bioskop on 27 December; on the 29th, one of the proprietors of the Folies Bergère took them to see the second evening of the Lumière Brothers' film-projections at the Salon Indien, situated in the basement of Paris's Grand Café (a far smaller projection-room than the Wintergarten Ballroom, seating only around 30 spectators, each of whom had paid one franc for admittance), and abruptly cancelled their contract, either due to international patent conflicts, or else because the Lumière Brothers had requested that cancellation. In addition, the technical superiority of the Lumière Brothers' 'Cinématographe' projector and the image-quality of their films was evident. Another engagement, at the Empire Theatre in London, was also annulled. But the Skladanowsky Brothers were able to tour extensively with the Bioskop, until September 1896, in Germany, Holland and Scandinavia, including occasions, as with an engagement at the Concerthaus in Hamburg in mid-December 1895, when only their films were shown, without an enveloping programme of variety-acts. As their tour progressed, it became apparent that the Skladanowsky Brothers were being rapidly surpassed by their competitors.

The Films Of The Skladanowsky Brothers

The films which the Skladanowsky Brothers projected at the Wintergarten Ballroom during November 1895, and on their subsequent film-tour until September of the following year, were almost exclusively sequences showing variety performers: together, their films assembled a slightly downmarket programme of variety acts to those appearing on the main stage of the Wintergarten, so that spectators exposed to those moving-images must have felt they were experiencing – through the medium of film, and at the evening's end – a concertinaed, phantasmatic variant of the live performances that had just finished. The Skladanowsky Brothers' films of the urban life of Berlin, recorded both in the peripheries and at the heart of the city, would be shot only in the following year, and projected only once, for their final screening-event in the city of Stettin in March 1897. And the brothers' very first film, shot as an experimental test on the rooftop of a building above the Schönhauser Allee avenue, belongs more to that second set of films than the first. In the film, Emil Skladanowsky is seen standing on the building's roof, dressed in a suit and tie, and holding his hat; he performs exaggerated corporeal gestures, pitched between gymnastics and clowning, alternately lifting each leg high into the air. The film camera is facing south, towards the centre of Berlin, in the opposite direction to the Skladanowsky Brothers' own local districts, as though intimating the direction in which their experiments were now taking them. The shadows cast by Emil Skladanowsky's figure indicate that the film was shot around midday, in direct sunlight. Behind his figure, a panorama is visible of factory and brewery chimneys, and large tenements, with the distinctive pointed steeple of the nearby Zionskirche church prominent in that cityscape. A notable strategy of early filmmakers was to focus their cameras on sites in which a maximal concentration of urban traces could be registered by their potential spectator, as with one of Le Prince's first films from 1888, of human and vehicle traversals of Leeds Bridge; with the Skladanowsky Brothers' film, the gesturing human body is in the foreground of the image, with the Berlin cityscape forming a cohering framework for it. But, as with Le Prince's film of Leeds Bridge, the Skladanowsky Brothers' first film was never projected, and was not included in the Wintergarten programme.(10) It survived only in fragments; the Prenzlauerberg Museum in Berlin possesses four celluloid frames, two of them exceptionally clear, with considerable detail of the urban panorama behind Emil Skladanowsky's figure, and the other two frames blurred and scratched, holding residues of damage in the form of scorch-marks from fire or smoke. The entire film had comprised 48 frames, so if it had been projected at 16 frames per second, it would have had a projection-duration of three seconds.

The eight short films projected at the Wintergarten Ballroom were all longer, comprising between 99 and 174 frames, and were each shown repeatedly, in loops. Shot in May 1895, two months before the Café Sello test-projections, they showed physical spectacles, dances and acrobatics. The first film to be projected each evening simulated an Italian peasants' dance, performed by two children; a further film depicted a wrestling contest featuring a celebrated bodybuilder and wrestler of the era, Eugen Sandow, fighting another wrestler named Greiner; the other films showed a boxing kangaroo, an acrobatics display, a human pyramid, a juggler, and a Russian cossacks' dance; finally, the film of the Skladanowsky Brothers themselves, appearing from either side of the screen, ended the programme. In some cases, the films held only a fragment of the complete action, which had either already begun before the camera started to record it, or else continued after the film had run-out. Other than their shared recording of contemporary variety performers, the programme's film-fragments held no linear or interlocking cohesion; together, the films formed a disjointed sequence of moments of eruptive and compelling spectacle, similar, in some ways, to the forms of 1960s European and American experimental cinema, such as the films of Kenneth Anger and Kurt Kren, which also possessed something of the aura of diabolical outlandishness, noted by the Wintergarten programme's press-reviews. In compiling and filming that programme, even before they had been commissioned to show their work at the Wintergarten, the Skladanowsky Brothers evidently devised a content which could be dependably well-received at a city-centre variety hall, and would allow their spectators, to the maximum possible extent, to recognise, situate and respond to the moving-images they were faced with. The brothers' specific choice of performers was clearly influenced, too, by their recent exposure to the Edison company's 'Kinetoscope' individual film-viewing machines, designed by William Dickson, which had been installed at another prominent Friedrichstrasse entertainment-venue, Castans Panoptikum, in March 1895, two months before the brothers shot their own films, and which showed similar physical feats and dances.

For the Wintergarten Ballroom projection, the Skladanowsky Brothers used film-strips of 44.5mm-wide unperforated Eastman-Kodak film-stock, which they meticulously cut and perforated by hand, so that it could run with the minimum disruption in front of the Bioskop's twin lens. The film-celluloid was also coated with a special emulsion, devised by Max Skladanowsky and applied with a brush. The films were all shot out-of-doors, either in the garden of the Café Sello or those of the venues in which the performers were then appearing, in direct sunlight, to achieve clarity and contrast. But most of the work of preparing both the shooting and projection of the films was undertaken in the Skladanowsky Brothers' own workshop, which functioned in that sense as an improvised and formative film-studio, prescient, in its artisanal dimensions, of the studio of the film-pioneer Georges Méliès, similarly installed on the urban periphery, in the eastern Paris suburb of Montreuil, and in which Méliès (who, like the Skladanowsky Brothers, attended the Lumière Brothers' film-projections at the Salon Indien in December 1895) began to shoot his hundreds of extravagant film-conjurations from March 1897 onwards. The Skladanowsky Brothers' workshop-studio also, in some ways, prefigures the spatial form of the far larger Weissensee film-studio, constructed in 1913 as a one-storey brick building in a Berlin district adjacent to that of their own workshop, and in which many of the seminal films of early German cinema, such as The Cabinet of Dr Caligari, were shot, before that studio abruptly went out of business in the late 1920s, in the face of competition from industrial-scale film-studios, with the derelict Weissensee film-studio building eventually being utilised, as it is today, as a sub-divided space for numerous artisans' workshops, in much the same way as the Skladanowsky Brothers' workshop-building operated in 1895. The brothers' first film, of Emil Skladanowsky's gestural movements against Berlin's urban panorama, was shot only a short distance from that workshop; access to the building's roof could be gained since a friend of the brothers operated his own business there.

The Skladanowsky Brothers' final films were shot during the later months of their projection-tour across Germany, Holland and Scandinavia, and also immediately after it, upon their return to Berlin. By that time, the original films shown at the Wintergarten Ballroom had worn out through over-use, and had become severely damaged (nothing now survives of the originally-projected films, only copies); in addition, the brothers had become aware that they urgently needed new films to seize the attention of their future audiences, and urban film-sequences fulfilled that desire. For their new films, they used 63mm-wide celluloid film-stock. In the centre of Berlin, they documented concentrations of horse-drawn vehicles and pedestrians in one of Berlin's main squares, the Alexanderplatz, and along the Unter den Linden avenue; in their own districts of industrial northern Berlin, they filmed at the Schönholz railway station, and also shot a further panorama from the rooftop of the building on which Emil Skladanowsky had performed his gymnastics movements, but this time with the camera facing in the opposite direction, northwards, focused on a busy street-corner, the Ecke Schönhauser, and without the foregrounded presence of a human figure. They also shot extremely brief 'fiction' films, depicting choreographed quarrels, such as one filmed in a public garden in Stockholm during the final phase of their projection-tour. In anticipation of future public screenings of their new films, Max Skladanowsky constructed a more sophisticated projector, the single-lens Bioskop-II, during the summer of 1896. But a second film-tour proved impossible to arrange. The Skladanowsky Brothers demonstrated their new projector and films to the Wintergarten's proprietors, with a view to being commissioned for a second engagement there, in February 1897, but were turned down in favour of rival film-exhibitors with more advanced projection-devices and films. The only engagement they could secure was in the provincial port-city of Stettin, north-east of Berlin, at the 2,000-capacity Zentrallhallen-Theater (later destroyed, like the Wintergarten, by British wartime bombing, along with most of what was then a German city, but became the postwar Polish city, Szczecin, its surviving German inhabitants expelled, and replaced by a population displaced from Polish territory annexed by the Soviet Union); the Skladanowsky Brothers showed their new city-films there for the only time, adding to that programme a new city-film shot and then rapidly developed in Stettin during the course of their two-week engagement. It was also the only occasion on which the brothers used their new projector, the Bioskop-II, for public screenings. On 31 March 1897, exactly seventeen months after their first Wintergarten screening, the brothers projected films for the last time.

The Oblivion And Memory Of The Skladanowsky Brothers

The Skladanowsky Brothers' brief film-career collapsed abruptly, in disarray and acrimony, on their return to Berlin from Stettin. In that highly regulated and bureaucratic era, expensive trade licences were required in Germany for such activities as public spectacles; the Berlin authorities declined to renew the brothers' license, which had expired on the last day of their engagement in Stettin, on the grounds that too many other film-exhibitors were now in operation (since the Wintergarten Ballroom projections, further film-screenings had become commonplace, and the first cinema-space in Berlin, devoted exclusively to the projection of films, had been opened in April 1896 by the film-entrepreneur Oskar Messter, in the backroom of a restaurant on the Unter den Linden avenue). In addition, the Skladanowsky Brothers would have had difficulty in paying for a new license even if it had been granted, since their long film-tour, with its cancellations and its necessity for sustained technological investment, had not been profitable. The two brothers, Max and Emil, fell out bitterly in June of that year, on their father's death, in a dispute over inheritance matters; Emil Skladanowsky was accused of attempting to defraud the other family members, and was ostracised by them. The quarrel was never resolved, and the brothers remained alienated from one another for the rest of their lives. In the following years, Max Skladanowsky switched his operations to the production of 'Daumenkino': small-format flick-books, which proved relatively lucrative. The flick-books' images were shot with a film-camera, with the resulting stills then compiled into handheld, elongated books, thumb-flicked to create continuous visual movement; the flick-books' contents ranged widely, from mild pornography to Berlin street-scenes and sequences showing political or aristocratic figures. Max Skladanowsky also created promotional flick-books to sell to manufacturing companies, such as one showing his daughter Gertrud drinking a meat-extract called 'Liebig's Fleischextract'.(11) Although he was not a pioneer of flick-books (they had been in existence since the 1860s), his original use of film-image sequences as their contents gave his products a distinctive aura, and he was able to make a living for at least a decade by producing and distributing them. During that period, he still had a residual interest in film-projection, and experimented in the years 1901-03 with ideas for colour film and three-dimensional technologies; however, he had no resources to exploit those experiments further, and with the decline of interest in flick-books, he instead established a workshop, in the industrial Prenzlauerberg district, for the production and sale of amateur photographic and filmmaking equipment. During the subsequent decades of obscurity, in which his film-projection innovations had been almost completely consigned to oblivion, he concentrated on taking photographs during long journeys on foot around northern Berlin, notably images of advertising hoardings announcing the building of new tenements in wastelands, as Berlin rapidly expanded northwards, and also panoramic photographs, often taken from the elevated summits of water-towers, documenting the traces of that urban expansion; at least some of those photographs were intended to be used for postcard-images. In some senses, Max Skladanowsky moved backwards in time after the dissolution of his seminal film-projection innovations, to the pre-filmic era, with his flick-book and photographic work. Emil Skladanowsky also returned to the kinds of spectacles he had been involved with before the Wintergarten film-screenings, notably managing tours of a successful water-theatre spectacle, before eventually gambling away all of his money.

Max Skladanowsky experienced an unexpected resurgence, and a return to public prominence, when the Nazi government came to power in Germany in 1933. Determined to recast all cultural lineages in order to highlight the pre-eminent role of Germany, the Nazi cultural authorities seized on the Wintergarten Ballroom film-projection event in order to elevate the now-elderly and semi-forgotten Max Skladanowsky to the status of a great German inventor. The propaganda minister Josef Goebbels appeared at a gala-evening dedicated to Max Skladanowsky at the lavish Atrium cinema in Berlin on 4 May 1933, and Hitler himself attended a private screening of the Skladanowsky Brothers' films in 1935.(12) Celebratory tours around Germany were arranged at which Max Skladanowsky spoke about his projection experiments and showed the 1896 city-films, which had since been transferred onto 35mm film. On the 40th anniversary of the Wintergarten projections, a month-long commemorative event was held at that venue, and Max Skladanowsky projected copies of the original 1895 films with the Bioskop; the estranged brothers were unwillingly brought together for the first time in almost forty years, for photographs in which each stares fixedly in opposed directions. Max Skladanowsky was fully complicit in the Nazis' support for his 1890s work, adding numerous 'Heil Hitler!' exclamations to his letters and also declaring the Bioskop to be an authentically German, non-Jewish invention; however, that support came at a moment when he was impoverished, following the collapse of his photographic business, and his enthusiasm for Nazism may have been, to some degree, feigned. The Nazi authorities were also ambivalent in their endorsement of Max Skladanowsky, in part because of his Polish family origins, but also because it was apparent that, since the mid-1920s, he had been clumsily reinventing the chronology of his filmmaking activities, backdating the rooftop film of Emil Skladanowsky to 1892, and also including the 1896 city-films among those screened at the Wintergarten in the preceding year. The Nazis' interest in him had declined by the time of his death in 1939, just after the outbreak of the Second World War; Emil Skladanowsky outlived his brother, and died shortly after the war's end, in 1945. During wartime British bombing-raids on Berlin, many of the Skladanowsky Brothers' filmmaking and film-projection artefacts, stored at the Reichsfilmkammer building, were incinerated; other materials, kept at the Skladanowsky family home in the district of Pankow, were destroyed during the chaotic house-to-house looting which took place once the invading Soviet army had reached northern Berlin in April 1945.

In the postwar era, the Pankow district was incorporated into the eastern, Soviet-controlled zone of Berlin. The surviving collection of the Skladanowsky Brothers' artefacts became dispersed. Max Skladanowsky's children sold much of that collection, including the Bioskop-I projector itself, to the East German state film-archive in 1966; an initial assessment of the material's condition categorised it as being 'in a terrible state'.(13) Much of that newly-acquired material was then sent to Paris on loan, in 1970, to the Cinémathèque Française, and was either forgotten or neglected there, before finally being returned to the now re-unified Germany in 1994; that material eventually became part of the German Bundesarchiv collection of film and theatre artefacts. The Bioskop-I projector has been exhibited since 1983 at the Potsdam Filmmuseum, close to Berlin. In Berlin itself, surviving artefacts of the Skladanowsky Brothers are held at the Deutsche Kinemathek film-centre, including copies of the films shown at the Wintergarten Ballroom in 1895, together with flick-books, travel-schedules, and press-books from the brothers' film-projection and 'Nebelbilder' tours (disordered counterparts, in some ways, to Muybridge's meticulous scrapbook-documentation of his own Zoopraxiscope tours). The Deutsches Technikmuseum displays the Skladanowsky Brothers' camera, used for the films shown at the Wintergarten, together with the Bioskop-II projector, both on loan from the Bundesarchiv collection. The Prenzlauerberg Museum, in the district of industrial northern Berlin where the Skladanowsky Brothers undertook their workshop-based experiments and shot their first film, holds many of their fragile glass-plate negatives, along with the photographs taken by Max Skladanowsky during his final decades.

At the time of celebrations for the centenary of public film-projection, in 1995, a new engagement with the Skladanowsky Brothers' work led to the restoration, from surviving copies or photographic images, of the programme of films shown at the Wintergarten Ballroom in 1895, undertaken, in part digitally, by the Optronik company in Potsdam; that programme of films was then shown in February 1995 at the Zoo-Palast cinema in Berlin, as part of that year's Berlin Film Festival. In the same year, Wim Wenders completed his semi-fictional film on the Skladanowsky Brothers' projections with the Bioskop, **Die Gebrüder Skladanowsky** (aka **Trick Of The Light**), directed in collaboration with film-students of the Munich Hochschule für Fernsehen und Film, and incorporating a sequence shot at the Potsdam Filmmuseum of the actor Udo Kier, playing Max Skladanowsky, operating the original, re-illuminated Bioskop projector; the film also includes extracts from interviews with Max Skladanowsky's youngest daughter, Lucie. At the film's end, a horse-drawn black carriage, carrying ghosts of the Skladanowsky family, disappears into the vast construction-site then engulfing the Potsdamerplatz in central Berlin. On the 70th anniversary of Max Skladanowsky's death, in 2009, the German Bundesarchiv completed its digitisation of images of its archival artefacts, and made them openly available online.(14)

The traces of the Skladanowsky Brothers in contemporary Berlin are simultaneously engrained, and erased: subject to oblivion, but also held within the profoundly shattered urban and filmic memory of the city, which compulsively projects its twin dynamics of illumination and catastrophe: a projection to be intimately experienced, in standing directly in front of the Bioskop, with its dual lens, one open, one closed.

Notes

(1) Alexandra Richie, *Faust's Metropolis*, Carroll and Graf, New York, 1998, p.221.

(2) Theo Fürstenau, *Max Skladanowsky: Deutsches Institut für Filmkunde: Sonderausgabe* (special issue), Deutsches Institut für Filmkunde, Wiesbaden, 1970, p.12.

(3) Joachim Castan, *Max Skladanowsky, oder der Beginn einer deutschen Filmgeschichte*, Füsslin Verlag, Stuttgart, 1995, pp.33-35.

(4) Fürstenau, p.10.

(5) Richie, p.212.

(6) Albert Narath, *Max Skladanowsky*, Deutsche Kinemathek, West Berlin, 1970, p.23.

(7) Castan, p.57.

(8) Narath, p.23.

(9) ibid, p.23.

(10) Castan, p.216.

(11) Narath, p.24.

(12) Castan, p.166.

(13) Undine Völschow, *Nachlass Max Skladanowsky*, Bundesarchiv, Koblenz, 1995, p.2.

(14) The images are on the website: www.bild.bundesarchiv.de

Thanks to the Potsdam Filmmuseum, the Prenzlauerberg Museum, the Deutsche Kinemathek Berlin, the Deutsches Technikmuseum Berlin, and the Bundesarchiv Film-Archiv Berlin. Translations from German are by the author.

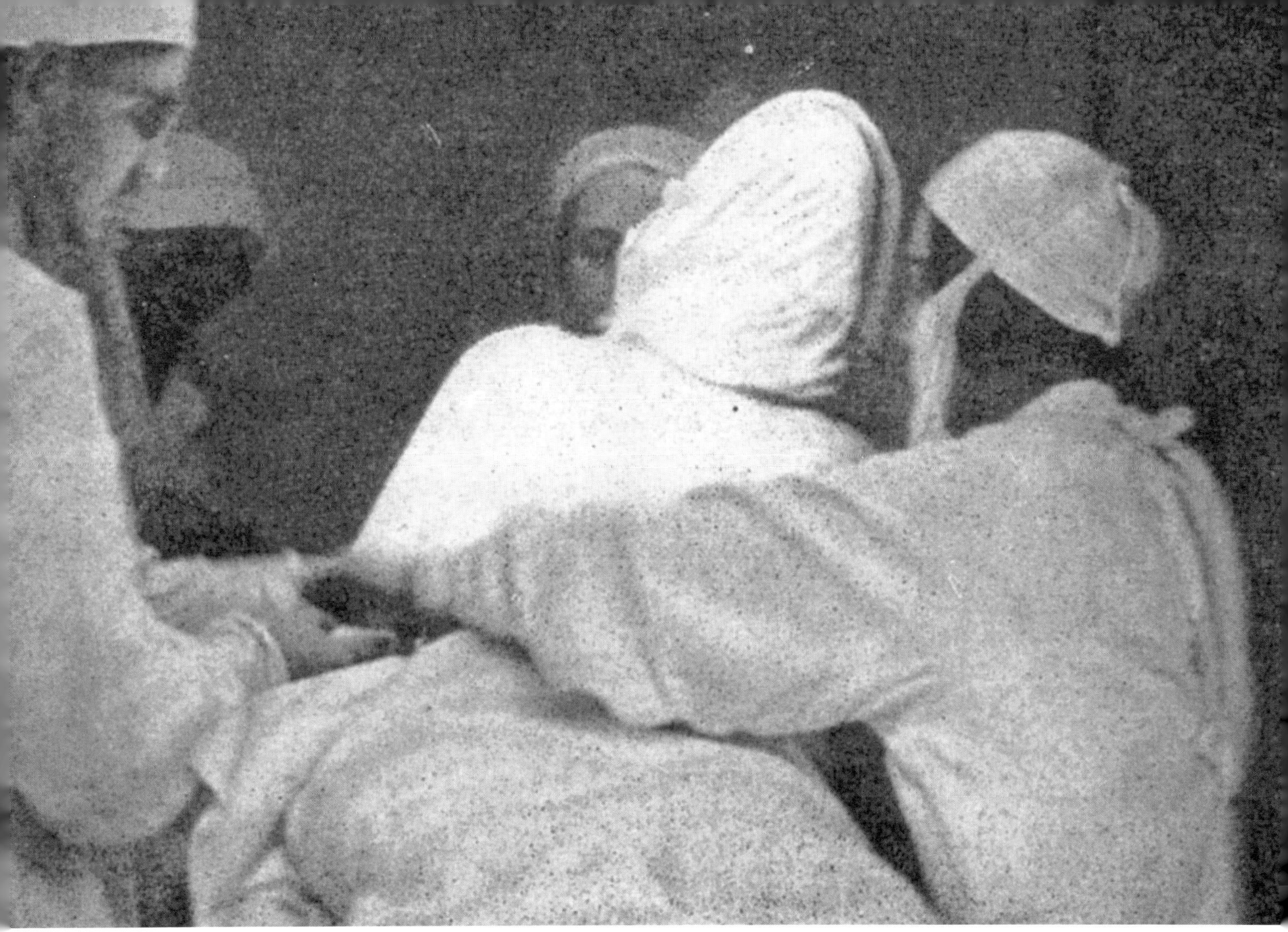

jean painlevé: "the corrective and reparative surgery of doctor claoué"

In 1930, scientific film-maker Jean Painlevé founded the Association for Photographic and Cinematic Documentation in the Sciences, along with Michel Servanne and Dr. Charles Claoué, a pioneer of cosmetic surgery (or *chirurgie esthétique*). That same year he made **Chirurgie Corrective Et Réparatrice Du Docteur Claoué**, a film of Claoué performing an operation to correct severe facial disfigurement, showing images of a mysterous, white-hooded patient before close-ups of scalpels slicing into tissue. The result is a warped plastic amalgam of atrocity, the macabre, and the profoundly poetic, resembling some prototype Surrealist horror movie. It's reported that Luis Buñuel, invited to the film's initial screening by Painlevé, had to look away in anguish and almost vomited. (Painlevé himself was far less squeamish; he once procured a severed human head for Claoué to practice upon, and on another occasion provided pickled human hands for Jean Vigo). Another surgical film which made a bilious impact when screened in Paris was Dr. Thierry de Martel's **Trépanation Pour Crise d'Epilepsie Bravais-Jacksonienne** (c.1940), a demonstration on a live (and conscious) patient of the electric skull-drill invented by Martel, who committed suicide during the Nazi occupation of the capital. Both films directly anticipate the bizarre and bloody clinical phantasma of Georges Franju's **Eyes Without A Face**, first masterwork of surgical horror cinema.

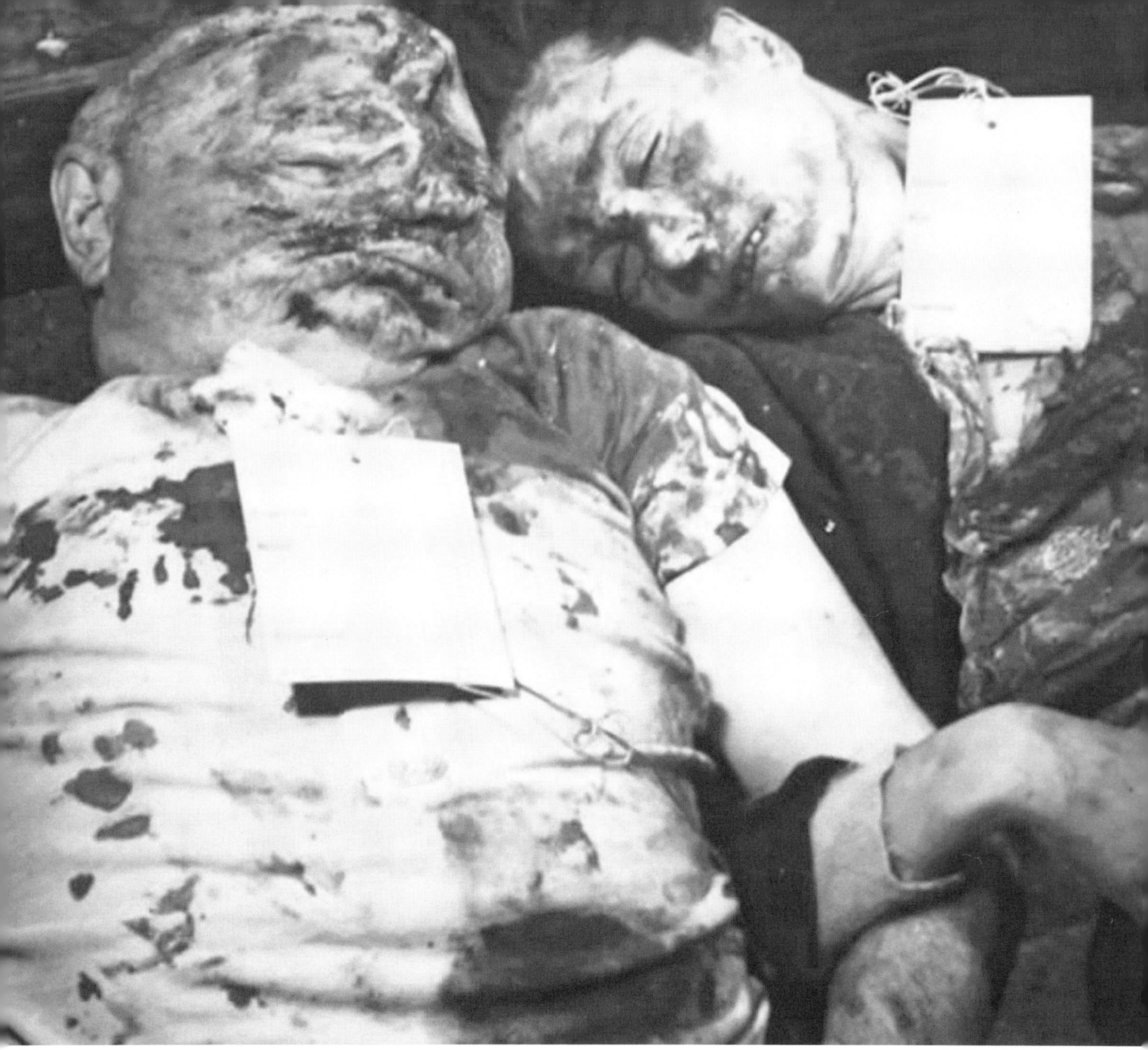

the corpse of mussolini

Italian dictator Benito Mussolini was arrested near Lake Como in April 1945, along with his hated mistress Claretta Petacci; the pair were severely beaten and shot the following day, and their corpses taken to the Piazzale Loreto in Milan. Here, they were strung up on girders, hanging upside down, and displayed to a baying mob who tried to inflict further damage to the already battered and lifeless bodies. These scenes were captured on film by US military cameramen, and form one of the most chilling, grotesque and violent episodes of the many which unfurled in the direct aftermath of WW2. The footage, which remained unseen until 1994, drew record audiences when screened on Italian television – along with grisly morgue film of an autopsy conducted after Mussolini's mangled corpse was cut down – under the title **Combat Film**, indicating the residual power and fascination wielded by the man known as *Il Duce*.

"the butcher's revolt": a film scenario by antonin artaud

Many of Antonin Artaud's commercial scenarios of the second half of the 1920s give the impression of a futile attempt to ingratiate himself with the formulaic mainstream film culture of the time, though each of them also contains an intermittently startling imagery of the body in extreme crisis. *The Seashell And The Clergyman* was the third of Artaud's scenarios, which number fifteen in all. By far the most extraordinary of all of the scenarios is the very last one, *The Butcher's Revolt*, which Artaud again intended to direct himself and for which he drew up an intricate – though, in its mathematical calculations, completely inaccurate – budget.

The Butcher's Revolt was written early in 1930, at the crucial point of crossover between the end of silent cinema and the innovation of sound cinema. The scenario possesses a far more cohesive narrative than *The Seashell And The Clergyman*; it even takes place in a specific location, around the Place de l'Alma in Paris. The principal figure in the scenario, introduced with irony by Artaud as "the madman", is in a dangerously obsessive state. While waiting to meet a woman in the street, he watches a carcass of meat fall from a speeding butcher's truck and becomes fascinated by the rapport between the texture of the meat and that of human flesh. He immediately provokes a brawl in a nearby café, and then takes part in a sequence of headlong chases (recalling those from Hollywood silent comedy films) which culminate in his arrival at a slaughterhouse and his humiliation there at the hands of the police. As with *The Seashell And The Clergyman*, the identity of the protagonist is volatile, and he experiences extremes of sensation, from joy to paralysing despair. The action of the scenario is powered by sudden transformations of space, punctuated by occasional outbursts of words, screams and noises.

In all of his scenarios before *The Butcher's Revolt*, Artaud had conveyed an adamant opposition to the introduction of sound into his film work. This was the moment of heated debate throughout Europe about whether the new technology of sound in cinema should be resisted or welcomed. In a lecture which he had delivered on 29 June 1929 at a cinema specializing in experimental work, the Studio 28 in Montmartre, Artaud declared:

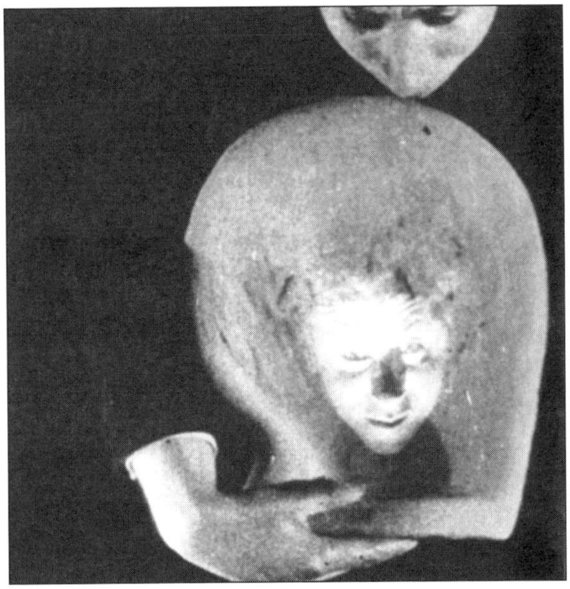

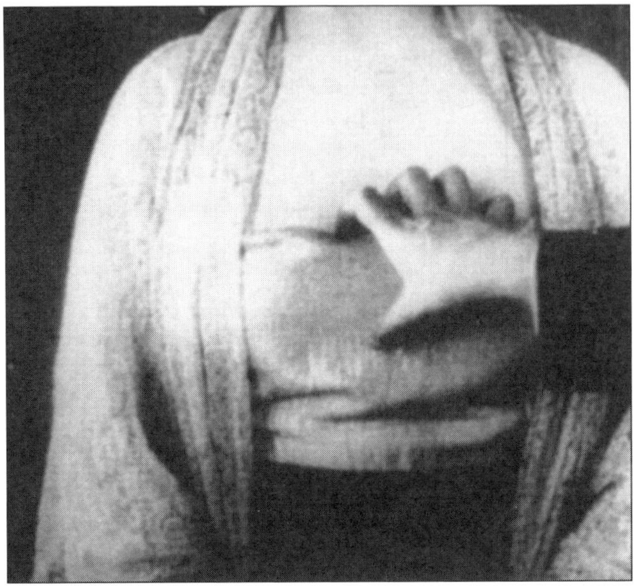

"There is no possible identification between sound and image. The image presents itself only in one dimension – it's the translation, the transposition of the real; sound, on the contrary, is unique and true, it bursts out into the room, and acts by consequence with much more intensity than the image, which becomes only a kind of illusion of sound."[1] Sound, for Artaud, would have to be separated from the image, in order for the image to maintain its own, autonomous resonances and impact. But the following year, with *The Butcher's Revolt*, Artaud attempted to come to terms with the growing inter-relationship of sound and image in cinema; he now viewed the element of mutual destructiveness which he perceived within this relationship as potentially valuable to his aims. He allowed a number of isolated and obsessive phrases (such as: "I've had enough of cutting up meat without eating it") into his scenario, typographically emphasizing them and enclosing them in black-bordered boxes. The words served as a way of imparting an abrupt emphasis to the visual imagery, which would, he believed, rebound from the image/sound collision with greater ferocity. The tense interaction of image, word and sound extended to Artaud's presentation of the scenario's content and its implications for spectatorship. In a note preceding the publication in June 1930 of his scenario in the literary periodical *La Nouvelle Revue Française*, Artaud summarised the content of the imagery: "eroticism, cruelty, the taste for blood, the search for violence, obsession with the horrible, dissolution of moral values, social hypocrisy, lies, false witness, sadism, perversity..." – all of this would be made explicitly visible for the spectator with "the maximum readability".[2] The vision of horror would itself become a visceral but disciplined language.

Artaud's strategy for sound in *The Butcher's Revolt* prefigures that used in his recording for radio, *To Have Done With The Judgement Of God*, eighteen years later. There, the sound effects – screams and rhythmic, percussive beatings – became inserted into Artaud's recited language of expulsion and refusal, with an immediate incision. In the recording, the violent physical gesture of the scream cuts across the escalating rush of the language's imagery in the way that, in Artaud's plan for *The Butcher's Revolt*, noise would have vitally lacerated the flow of the visual images. Similarly, in Artaud's notebook drawings of the mid-1940s, the entangled arrangements of texts and images are often seared by a sudden gesture of obliteration – a pencil stroke that abruptly makes its trajectory across the page, simultaneously reinforcing the powerful visual emanation of language and image as it cancels them.

In *The Butcher's Revolt*, the primacy accorded by Artaud to the image and its spatial presence broke with the predominant film style of the time, which consisted of a kind of filmed theatre that emphasized

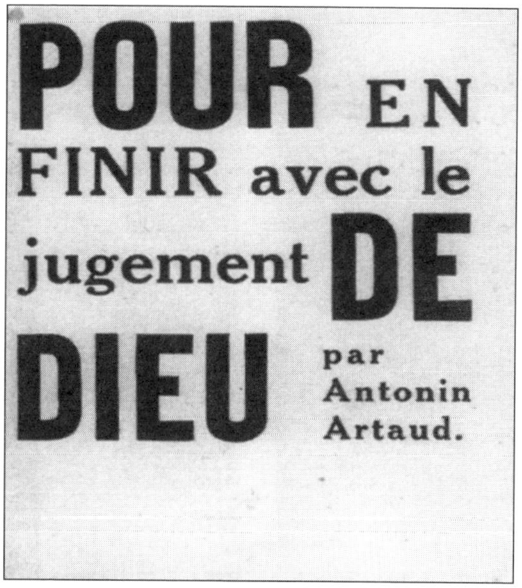

psychological dialogue and the passage of time. In his note about *The Butcher's Revolt*, Artaud stressed the spatial quality of the reinforced sound which he would employ: "The voices are in space, like objects."[3] Space is a crucial element in Artaud's conception of film. There is a constant preoccupation with expanding and manipulating the spatial dimension while erasing or reducing time. The passage from film frame to frame is an especial danger in Artaud's perception; each image must be emphasised to such intensity that the intervening passage of time between the images can be suppressed to its maximum degree. In his "Theatre of Cruelty" of the early 1930s, there is a parallel concern with spatial movement: the actor's gesture must burn itself out into space with unique immediacy and impact, and must not be repeated in time. The very first of Artaud's film scenarios, *Eighteen Seconds*, from 1924, evokes the thoughts of an actor during the period of eighteen seconds between the moment at which he looks at his watch and the moment at which he shoots himself in the street. A complex sequence of images and spatial mutations is arranged into a condensed period of time, which would then have to be expanded to an hour or two of cinematic duration. Since the process of representation operates for Artaud on a temporal level, on which sound and image are repeated and disseminated, his determination to introduce a spatial rather than temporal element into film sound signalled a denial of the movement towards diminishment and repetition which any completed, represented art object makes. In Artaud's conception of cinema, the presence of the human body in which the film has its axis must be immediate and dense. It is likely that Artaud was aware of a precedent to this aspect of his theory, in the form of the Italian Futurist film manifesto of November 1916, which had demanded "polyexpressiveness" and proposed "filmed unreal reconstructions of the human body".[4] With a scenario such as *The Butcher's Revolt* that projected the amalgamation of diverse, volatile physical elements into a spatially flexible and eruptive structure, Artaud was envisaging a cinema which – like all of his subsequent visual and aural work – was acutely resistant to representation.

Notes

1. Antonin Artaud, extract from lecture (1929), *Oeuvres Complètes*, Volume III, page 377.
2. Antonin Artaud, untitled note (1930) accompanying *La Révolte Du Boucher*, in *Oeuvres Complètes*, Volume III, page 54.
3. ibid, page 54.
4. Film manifesto entitled "The Futurist Cinema", originally published in the journal *L'Italia Futurista*, Rome, issue 9, 11 November 1916, and reproduced in part in the catalogue *Film As Film*, Hayward Gallery, London, 1979, pages 79–80.

sorcery and cinema

You hear it repeated everywhere that the cinema is in its infancy and that we are present only at its first babblings. I have to say that I don't understand this kind of perception. The cinema is arriving at an already advanced stage of the development of human thought and it benefits from this development. Certainly, the cinema is a means of expression that isn't yet materially fully formed. You can imagine, for example, a number of innovations capable of giving the film camera a stability and movement which it currently doesn't have. We will one day probably have multi-dimensional cinema, even colour cinema. But these are secondary elements and won't add much to what is the core of cinema itself, and which makes cinema a language in its own right, on a par with music, painting or poetry. I've always recognized in cinema an essential quality of secret movement and of material images. Cinema possesses a distinctive element of surprise and mystery which you never find in the other arts. It's certain that every image – however dry, however banal – arrives on the screen transformed. The smallest detail, the most insignificant object carries a meaning and a charge of life which belong exclusively to them – and which extend beyond the value and meaning of the images themselves, and beyond the thought that they translate or the symbol that they carry. Because cinema isolates objects, it gives them a life which is separated and which becomes more and more independent as it detaches itself from the banal sense of objects. Some leaves, a bottle, a hand: they are all animated with a sort of animal life, which demands to be put to use. The film camera creates deformations, makes extraordinary use of the things which you give it to record. The image disappears and at that moment, a detail appears which you had never imagined, igniting with intense force, and heading off in search of the impression you were yourself searching for. There is in cinema a kind of physical intoxication which communicates the movement of images directly to the brain. The mind is set into upheaval, beyond all representation. This hidden power of images tracks down potential forces in the depths of the mind that have never before been activated. The cinema essentially reveals an occult life and puts us into direct contact with it. You have to know how to understand that occult life. A play of superimpositions works to reveal secrets that are in turmoil in the depths of the mind. The raw cinema, taken exactly as it is – in the abstract – disgorges an atmosphere of trance which is eminently capable of revelations. To make it only tell stories, or record exterior actions, deprives cinema of the best of its resources and obstructs its most profound aim. This is why cinema seems to me to have been created above all to express the elements of thought, the interior of consciousness – not so much by the play of images than by something harder to seize, which directly restores the matter of images to us, without any intermediation, without any representation. Cinema has appeared at a time when human thought itself is at a watershed moment – at the precise moment when language has become exhausted and has lost the power of its symbols, and when the human mind has grown tired with representational games. Lucidity is not enough – it only serves to situate a world that is exhausted to breaking-point. Whatever can be clearly perceived is immediately accessible, but whatever is immediately accessible simply forms an empty appearance of life. We're starting to realize that this life – which is too well-known and has lost its symbols – is not the whole of life. The contemporary moment is a ripe one for all sorcerers and saints: a time more beautiful than has ever before existed. A substance which was previously unperceived is now taking a physical form and trying to reach the light of day. Cinema brings us close to that physical substance. If cinema wasn't created to transmit dreams and everything that waking life classifies as

belonging to the domain of dreams, then cinema wouldn't exist. It would be no different to theatre. But cinema, this direct and immediate language, has no need of heavy, slow logic in order to live and expand. Cinema must become closer and closer to the fantastic – and we see more and more that the fantastic is, in reality, the real; otherwise, cinema will die – or, more exactly, it will become just another art form, like painting, like poetry. What is certain is that most forms of representation have had their day. Paintings, however good they may be, have for a long time only reproduced the abstract. So it's not just a question of choice – there's isn't a cinema which represents life on one hand, and a cinema which represents the workings of the mind on the other. Life – or what we call life – is going to become inseparable from the mind. A profound mental terrain is starting to break through to the surface. The cinema, better than any other art form, is capable of tracking the movements of this terrain – since moronic order and habitual clarity are the enemies of cinema.

The Seashell And The Clergyman is involved in this research into a subtle kind of order, into a hidden life which I've wanted to render as believable and real as the other kind of life.

To understand this film, all you need to do is to look deeply into yourself. Devote yourself to this examination: an objective, material and attentive examination of the internal, separated SELF – which until now has been the exclusive domain of the 'Illuminated'.

Artaud wrote this essay in the Café Terminus in Paris at the time of the shooting of **The Seashell And The Clergyman**, in August–September 1927. –Stephen Barber

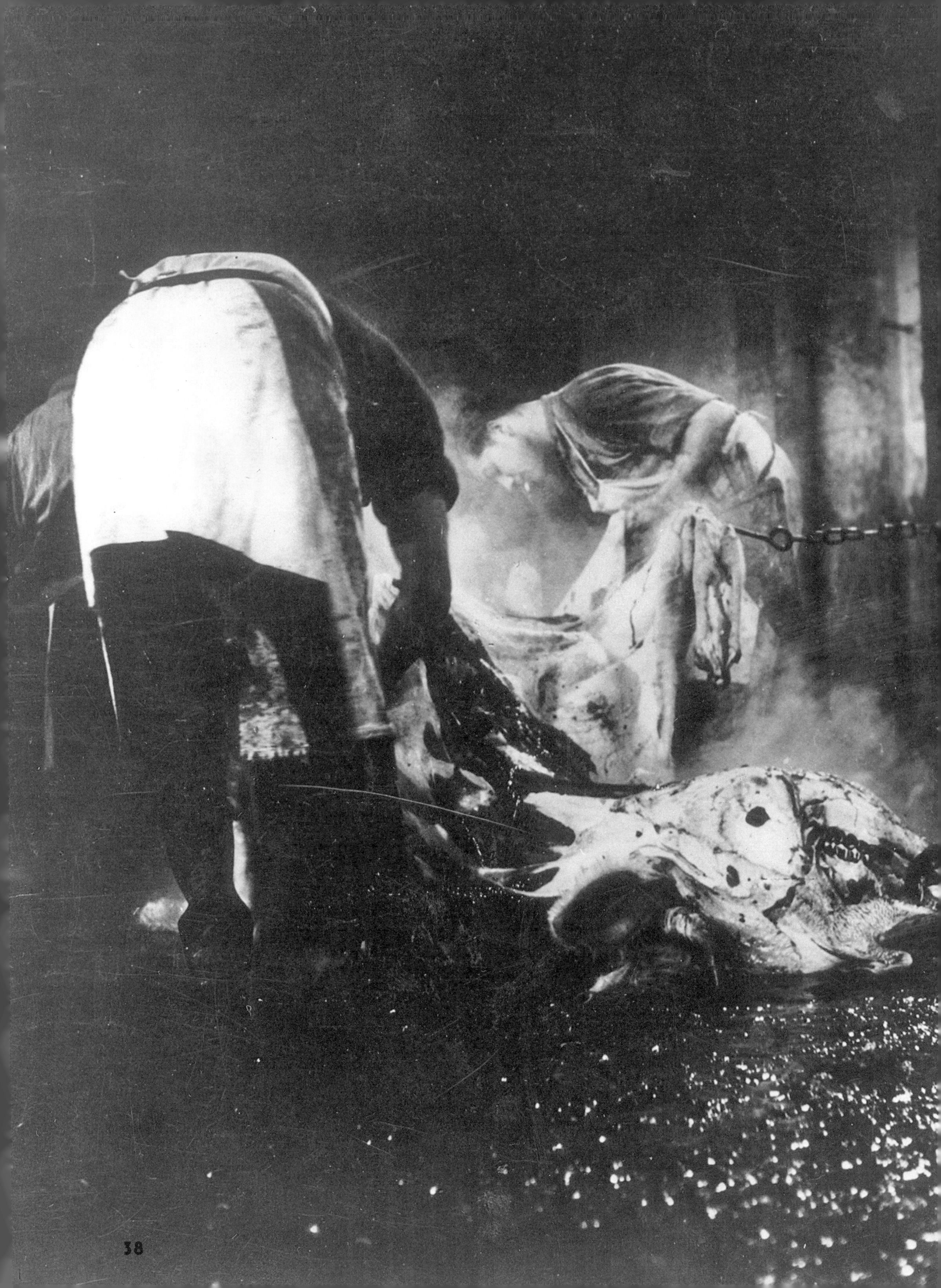

georges franju: "le sang des bêtes"

In a wasteland, old goods are heaped for sale. Grey rubble and grey sky stretch away beyond a dining-room table in solid oak, and an electric lamp hangs from the branches of a tree. Each item remembers, recreates, the room around it. Furnishing and setting between them create a double image of house and horizon, akin to certain paintings of Magritte.

A building rears up before the camera, its bleak brick asserting all the utilitarian impersonality of the nineteenth century. It might be a prison, a warehouse, a cotton mill, a pickle factory.

Among the tools of its trade are the poleaxe, the spike, the humane killer, tools which its craftsmen wield with skill and pride.

A meek white carthorse rears back under the impact of a humane killer, stumbles, kneels, keels over. A spike is plunged deep into its neck, and a torrent of blood gushes steaming forth. Round the prone bulk men bustle and hack, and in a few moments the carcass is dismembered.

To paralyse their reflexes (for threshing and flailing spoils meat), and secondarily to anaesthetise them, cows have long steel spikes banged through their skulls into their brains.

Calves with their throats cut judder about so obstinately that their kicking heads send the pans of their hot blood skidding and slopping across the tiled floor; men have to restrain their posthumous vivacity.

A butcher saws through a cow's hanging carcass in the time it takes for the town hall clock to strike mid-day.

Knee-deep in blood, the craftsmen sing popular songs, among them the Charles Trenet hit, *La Mer*.

Sheep are dismembered, their heads and feet put on separate stacks. Row upon row of legs kick furiously.

The film ends by returning us to a city whose grey, inarticulate stone is infused with the sadness of all industrial concentrations.

The film's form is not simply that of prologue, 'body' and coda, but also that of thesis (the sad city), a terrible antithesis (the slaughterhouse), and the synthesis (the coalescence, in our minds, of the two).

This schema fairly summarises the film's structure, but if the last statement closes in on us with teeth like a mantrap's it's because, during the central section, Franju has found formal or poetic pretexts to cut away from the slaughterhouse to the city which it feeds. It's not simply that Franju has a delicate ear for contrasts, nor simply that, with macabre showmanship, he avoids piling shock upon shock, without relief, in case he eventually stunned, or even inured, us. These formulations suggest that every shot that's not violent is merely a breathing-space between those that are. But the 'intermediate' shots have two positive functions. If Franju intersperses the paroxysmic sequences with asides of an elegiac and/or ironic nature it is to resensitize the spectator, and therefore his response to violence; it is with his finer fibres that he bears the shock. The cutaways repoeticize, they reintellectualize, and they reassert that the slaughterhouse and the city are an entity, like spider and spider's web. As the virtuoso butcher hacks at the cow's hung carcass, and the clock strikes twelve, shots of various aspects of the city synchronize with the strokes. After the final disposal of the white horse, we return to the outside world to see a flock of white sheep being led across a canal: 'their bleating is like the singing of hostages' (if the comparison seems slightly forced, it is no doubt less so to those who have heard hostages' songs in just such streets). Two nuns walk up to the slaughterhouse gates, their headdresses like seagulls, knock on the door and beg for offal. At first

sight, the film's climactic violence is its positive pole, the quieter shots the negative. But, from another angle, it is the quieter shots which constitute the film's, and the spectator's, home key.

Franju cheerfully explains the secret of his film's opening. 'In fiction, fantasy is usually obtained by giving the artificial (studio decor, etc.) the appearance of reality. In our films we set out to restore to documentary realism its actual quality of apparently artificial decor. We managed it by shooting buildings from directly in front (like the Moulin de Panton) or else we chose houses with sharp profiles (at the Port du Flandre) and avoided any hint of depth... Whether in the business of the barge emerging "in" the wasteland... like a theatre flat, or with those trees which look like theatre props, we were constantly preoccupied with expressing the plastic character of the decor, and we often waited for several days for the weather to be simultaneously diffuse (misty) and dense in the sky, or else for everything to be lit up with that particular, local colour which strikes one as a freak of the sunlight...'

The violent scenes are no less sensitively observed (although the subject matter is likely to pre-empt the spectator's conscious attention). 'The choice of the month of November for shooting the interiors was dictated by the fact that at this season of the year the animals are slaughtered by electric light, and the blood steaming in the glacial cold of the scalding bays allowed us, despite all the technical problems, to compose our images...'

This unvarying sensitivity, not simply to aesthetics, but to reality, enables a double image, analogous to that of the home-wasteland, to reappear in the heart of the violence: in Henri Agel's words, 'the ordering of the dismemberments takes on an almost ritual character, the stunned horse falls in a curtsey, while the killers, bathed in vapours of blood, seem to officiate...'

'It's for the sake of aesthetic realism that I chose a child-like girl's voice, confidential and lightly overcast like the weather, to speak over the exteriors the rigorous, moving and sometimes ironic commentary of Jean Painlevé.' It's not altogether a coincidence that Nicole Ladmiral, who speaks the commentary, also plays Chantal in Bresson's **Journal d'un Curé de Campagne**, for a common personality often implies a common mood; and the effect of the grey, unemphatic voice is akin to Bresson's when he requires his actors to speak their lines without responding to the meaning in them. But for neither Franju nor for Bresson's case is this actually expressionless – the voice has its key, its mood; the fact of a girl's voice is itself a statement, its tone of quietly sad, passive matter-of-factness is another: anything more would 'beautify the beautiful', and lose the mesmerism of the factualness.

Similarly, in the heart of the atrocious, one doesn't merely note, one is profoundly affected by the deftness and speed of the butchers; we see it so clearly that, for all the crosscurrents in us of (misdirected) anger and tragic irony, we can share their legitimate pride in their skill, do justice to the moral neutrality of their song, to their own qualities as victims. The butchers never become scapegoats, and so refract our disquiet back from them to the system of which the audience is also a part.

Most spectators remember the film as an intense experience, but usually, it seems, in a very abstract way. They have a lively memory of its overall effect, but ask them to describe specific scenes, and they can remember only one or two – usually the white horse, presumably because it possesses overtones of iconographic sentimentality, and because it is the film's first shock. Very few people remember from films, or novels for that matter, more than a mood and a few 'snapshots', but it's surprising that the same amnesia should operate in the case of a film so vivid that it brings some people near the point of fainting. One would expect the 'horror' images to be branded upon the mind. Perhaps this forgetting is a sort of fainting. Perhaps, too, the fact that the film is remembered emotionally rather than visually suggests that its effect is as much a matter of structure and counterpoint as of raw visual realism *per se*. Sometimes, too, people remember the peripheral shots, where the horror imbues and is dilated by the everyday, where the Paris skies rumble with ominous gradations of grey, and its sullen mass flickers with the sadly starting flocks of birds.

The constant interpenetration of finesse and violence so attunes our imagination as to impregnate with special meanings scenes on which no comment need even be implied. The shot of the sheep crossing the bridge into the slaughterhouse, scenting blood, reluctant to enter, but reassured by 'leaders' specially planted by their shepherds, can't but recall the words of the 23rd Psalm. The Lord may be one's shepherd, he may feed one and make one down to lie in green pastures, but he may also lead one into clean slaughterhouses. Blake objected to shepherds who shear the faithful of their fleece, but even stronger objections are appropriate for a God whose intentions are to reduce one to the spiritual equivalent of meat. In any case, do shepherds really love their flock (except collectively), would they lay down their life for it (except inadvertently)? Similarly, Agel seems to have missed the point about the sacrificial overtones to the slaughter. Given Franju's anti-clericalism, it's hardly likely to be, as Agel's description suggests it can be taken as being, that butchers are in a sense the priests of life's eternal tragedy, that the animals are, in a kind of pantheistic communion, sacrifically allowing their life-force to be transubstantiated into man, who, as a spiritually higher creature, is capable of grasping God on behalf of the lower animals too. On the contrary: Franju's parable is a warning of the folly of all blind, habitual obedience to those set in authority over us, for our own good, of course. The overtones don't transform the executioners into priests; the metaphor flows the other way; next time you see a priest officiating at the altar, think of him as a butcher. The vibrations of the scene strike not only at Christianity, but at any number of religions or, indeed, at man's religious impulse, centred as it is on those ceremonies of sacrifice which seek to deny death, to mystify injustice into self-sacrifice, to repudiate responsibility (scapegoat symbolisms), to attain an immortal life which is only an immunity from life (i.e. the protection of death), to enjoy a mystic 'community' which doesn't exist, whereas the seas of blood through which the singing butchers stride certainly do exist.

The hacking of the carcass while the clock strikes provoked two critics to cite John Donne. For Alan Lovell, 'the set of cutaways to "our" city is an exact filmic equivalent of John Donne's "No man is an island".' And for this writer, '"For whom the bell tolls" is given a chilling insouciance. The bell creates a dramatic solemnity, akin to a crucifixion (the hanging carcass). But instead of darkness at noon it's business as usual, or a quiet siesta while one's digestive juices soak up that steak.' The episode is a classic example of montage in the Eisensteinian sense: not because of its quick cutting, which is montage only in the debased Hollywood sense, but because the thesis (the carcass) and the antithesis (the city) produce a synthesis which is as abstruse as the phrases of a metaphysical poet. Even this dialectic yields too simple an account: for beside hung carcass/crucifixion come other 'pairs': axe-strokes/clock's strokes and so on. The meaning lies not in one dialectic, but in several, which don't so much add up to an eventual synthesis, but horizontally transform the values of individual terms. Indeed this revision of dialectics might usefully be transferred from poetic to political theory. And, to return to Eisenstein, montage consists, not in the juxtaposition of objects to produce one single meaning, but in the juxtaposition also of all their associations, including those imported by stylistic nuance, producing a bunch of meanings.

Franju is not so ascetic as to resist an extrinsic comment when it doesn't disturb his effect. Thus it is only those connoisseurs of movie technique who, in seeing a film, carefully study the synchronization of sight and sound, who will notice that the commentary is talking about nuns while an image shows the excrements of a cow. Franju's humour has its peasant flavour. But only those comments are made which, while appealing to his *amis inconnus*, often assert a blasphemous implacability against that sentimental and undeserved respect for the feelings of the religious which so often reduces criticism of Christianity to something like a confession of respectful admiration. But he allows himself only those comments which, as self-effacing as certain cryptograms in music, assert no false emphasis against the film's principle impetus, which is directed at the slow dilatation of appearances until, as tender, as clumsy and as surreal as a new-born calf, reality appears.

The perils of the opposite course, of a conspicuous and insistent commitment, are exemplified by a Czechoslovak picture called, in Britain, **Isn't Life Wonderful?**, or variations on that title. Its attack on the complacencies of bourgeois optimism is carried out by every effect of ironic contrast: 'Blue Skies' sung by Bing Crosby, 'C'est si Bon' by Louis Armstrong, overlaid on shots of concentration camps, the starving poor, and so on. In structure, the effect is exactly that of Franju's use of *La Mer* over a sea of blood. But there are two important differences. The butcher's song naturally arises from, exists in the situation itself; it isn't dragged in. Czechoslovakian contrasts, taken from here, there and everywhere, immediately take on a philosophical-political sphere of reference; being knockdown polemic, they mobilise all our polemical defences. Furthermore, the rhetorical means being almost more obvious than the ends, one is likely to resent the hectoring tone even if one agrees with it. With a whoop of triumph, all one's sales resistance seizes on its imprecision. One may agree with the attack on pop music, or on the commercial media, or American culture in general, and Western culture in general. No doubt it is extremely wicked of us to allow ourselves even one second's relaxation while suffering is going on anywhere in the world, and we ought to let our standard of living drop like a stone while we buckle to the task of helping Oxfam's teeming millions. But my immediate reaction is to reflect that the film might have been less facile and more disturbing if its expressions of our complacency had also featured high culture: Toscanini, in fine style, conducting cannons and napalm-bursts, Fonteyn-Nureyev tripping the light fantastic in *Swan Lake* while refugees tramp along dusty endless roads, the fine eloquence of Olivier compared with the cost of silence that is the real face of suffering, and so on. But however you shift the terms the contrasts are facile and static, because they're mere contrast. Much closer connections are needed before all the associations of each element can be brought into contact and so create the myriad subtle contrasts which result in poetry.

For all that, **Le Sang Des Bêtes** can hardly be summed up, as it is constantly summed up, as a poetic vision of a slaughterhouse. For 'poetic vision' implies that there are un-poetic, common-sensical, matter-of-fact views of slaughterhouses. And it carries the further implication: 'of course, Franju is a very sensitive person, a poet – naturally, he would feel things acutely; but all that sensitivity is poetic and visionary, you know; it's all a matter of cultural ornaments, not of real life.' The corollary of this approach to life is the sort of poem one might

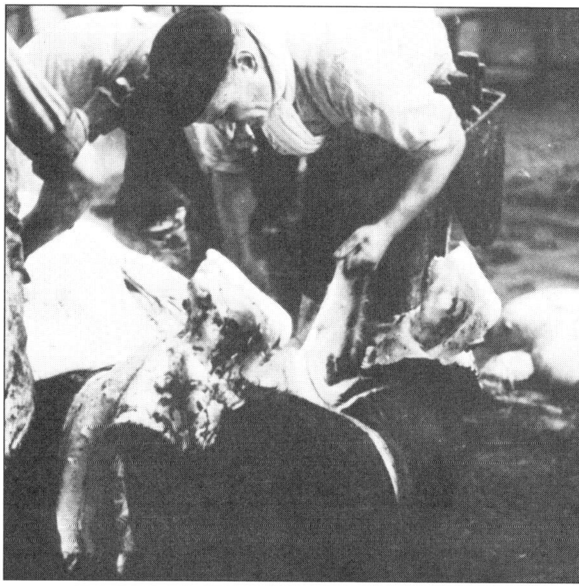

find in certain literary journals – something written by a poet-tourist who, visiting a slaughterhouse, immediately thought 'I really mustn't lose this opportunity of writing a poem; after all, a slaughterhouse is a very poetic place', and stands around noting sensitive metaphors in his little book. What comes out is a densely textured little poem which richly deserves its high mark: say 991/2 out of 100. But a mark is all it deserves. One recalls Stephen Spender, gazing at unemployed men begging in railway halls and vowing, 'No, I shall weave no tracery of pen-ornament/To make them birds upon my singing tree', to which the appropriate answer is, no doubt, to touch one's cloth cap and mutter, 'Cor, ta, guv'nor, yer a real toff.' The very metaphor is as neat a bit of euphuistic tracery as anything since Lyly. One could write a thesis on the peculiar passivity implied in that Spender-Auden era mannerism 'Let...' (in this case 'the wrong cry out as raw as wounds'), as if the world was somehow run by a moral destiny equivalent to their old headmaster, whom they, like radical fifth formers, were petitioning. Most depressing of all is the relentless dissolution of everybody and everything into a *pointillisme* of metaphors, similes, and abstract emotive words: the result of the sensitive style is to render the unemployed thoroughly abstract and substitute for them an intricate tracery of abstractions which has the minor qualities of a political Georgianism, including moral pathos, but makes a solid, prosaic contact impossible.

If one imagines a slaughterhouse poem along similar lines, it's easy to imagine how our poet-tourist, more concerned, really, with his poetry than with his raw material – a symptomatic phrase – multiplies the mental and verbal suggestions, but loses the real massiveness of the main business of slaughterhouses, which is slaughter. This isn't to say that the onlooker's reality isn't a reality, obviously it is, nor is it to say that one can't proceed, as Franju has, from observation to empathy and insight. But it's a much less interesting reality, indeed, it can be a 'confusionist' reality, than the reality which includes both the objective and the subjective realities of slaughter. The attempt to subsume both aspects of the subject will inevitably involve one in deploying all the resources of poetic sensitivity.

Conversely, the best poetry about reality has all the prosaic virtues, works *with* the prosaic, and a step towards a new classical language is being taken with the evolution of a new poetic prose *à la* Trocchi, Kerouac, etc. For the butchers, the slaughtering is all in the day's work, so the Hamlets of this particular Prince of Denmark are the animals, for whom it's all a matter of life and death, or rather, of death. It's true that they don't know what hit them, and that the fact that 'life must go on' makes the dead uninteresting. We can all feel in ourselves the seeds of that rather terrifying viewpoint whereby the dying or the old hardly matter, whereby their feelings lie as lightly on the scale as their future, a valuation to which the old themselves often subscribe. Hence the importance of works of art which insist that even 'dead-end' experiences, even the muddled panic in a pig's brain as his misgivings intensify and suddenly his throat gets more or less deftly sliced, matter from an objective point of view. Hence the importance of not allowing pure poetry to settle for that sensitive impressionism which, while dealing admirably with all sorts of peripheral nuances and reflections, can no more catch the central shocks of the experience than you can catch a charging rhinoceros in a shrimping-net.

To some extent, the trap is easier to fall into in literature than in the cinema, since literature has to reconstruct reality from a network of abstract equivalents, words, whereas the cinema can home in more directly on the concrete and the physical. But the achievements of literature, and the pitfalls of cinema, can be symbolized by the intensely poetic prose of Hardy, or any bad film, i.e. nine films out of ten. And there is no reason in the media themselves why literature should not match or even surpass, for example, Franju's quiet presentation of the tools and tricks of the butcher's trade. Indeed, the poetry of practicality which is so often so dreadfully lacking from the spectrum of current poetry is inherent in certain technical manuals for nurses, undertakers, butchers and others whose occupations carry tabus because of their disturbing, that is, poetic reality. For example, the chapters on slaughterhouse techniques in Frank Gerrard's *Meat Technology* (Leonard Hill, London, 1964) present a somewhat idealized picture, in that the account of how to do it well hardly suggests the wild messes that occur when it's not well done, and in that it's emotionally aseptic. But, poetically read, the asepticism is itself an irony, and the techniques give some insight into the anatomical infrastructure of the subjectively unspeakable, as well as carrying a respect for the practical process which gets lost in a culture whose frame of reference too rarely leaves that of the white-collar worker.

We may already have seen decapitated chickens running around as if looking everywhere for their heads, but here, locked as we are in a cinema, with only a succession of death-images to contemplate, death ceases to be a definite boundary, for the nervous system clearly has its doubts. We are gripped by the screen's tight image into an intensive identification with the dying, an identification probably more intense than we would feel if we were walking round an actual slaughterhoues, where we would need to keep a mask on our faces and could easily look away from, or not even notice, those details to which Franju relentlessly drags our attention. Now we cannot but doubt the hangman's usual apologia, to the effect that hanging (or gassing, or electrocuting) is all but painless, if not actually enjoyable. What's sauce for the goose is sauce for the human animal too, and the posthumous agitations eerily caricature, and reverse, the usual argument about souls. Maybe the space within our minds is infinitely larger than the space within our skulls, but our minds' desires and actions are firmly rooted in the biological mind-body warp constituted by our carcasses, by the lumps of meat which swell proudly beneath our shirts and strut around in our trousers. These butchers' knives cut theology's throat, and leave it bleeding to death at the back of our minds.

Given Franju's connections with the scientific film, it's fitting that the commentary for the first of his 'grand series' of documentaries should be written by Jean Painlevé, whose documentaries on vampire bats, sea-horses and sea-urchins and other bizarre modalities of the life-force plunge us into consciousnesses stranger than our wildest dreams. To see these films is to dream ourselves into biological warps which reveal our world as a reticulation of other worlds as eerie as anything in Philip José Farmer's 'The Lovers', Theodore Sturgeon's 'Venus Plus X' or Nicolas Devil's 'Les Aventures de Saga'. What seems in retrospect even eerier is that we could ever have thought this world was familiar. No doubt your pet dog or your pet snake really loves you, in the fully human sense of the word, but what, concretely, goes on in his mind? What is the image of your dog's recognition of you?

Painlevé's science-fact can be contrasted to science-fiction, just as the natural sciences can be contrasted with metaphysics. Milton has been called an ancestor of science-fiction, in so far as he allows himself to speculate upon the digestive processes of angels. But he had never seen an angel and was working it all out from those rules which appeared to operate in the world he knew. Rationalism = extrapolation = metaphysics. The natural sciences reverse the approach. Extrapolation may yield a hypothesis, but a hypothesis is all it is until you have caught your angel and put, if not salt on its tail, at least radioactive tracers in its food, and also conducted a post-mortem. Materialism = empiricism = hypotheses. Science-fiction is the metaphysics of an age which doesn't believe in metaphysics, just as poetry is spilled religion. Indeed, science-fiction is a contemporary form of poetic myth, and its relation to science-fact (which inventions Wells predicted, etc.) is the least important thing about it. Of course science-fact and science-fiction can impregnate each other, just as poetic myth is most impressive when it's 'married' to a believed cosmogony. And this is why it isn't as perverse as it may seem to indicate the progression Franju-Painlevé-Farmer, that is, the progression from Franju's *poesie matérialiste* (a phrase of Maurice Nadeau's about Prévert first applied to Franju by Freddy Buache) to *poésie scientifique* and then *poésie science-fiction.* **Le Sang Des Bêtes** is to *poesie science-fiction* as **Hiroshima Mon Amour** is to **L'Année Dernière A Marienbad**. The first pair concern other modalities of consciousness as the latter pair concern the human mind's grip on memory and reality.

Painlevé's **Les Assassins De L'Eau Douce**, which shows myriad forms of freshwater life devouring one another assiduously, to the soundtrack of 'thirties swing-music, reveals that your humble pond is, among other things, a gaily relentless Auschwitz, that assassinating to absorb is also an essential link of being, a form of community; **Le Sang Des Bêtes** is a parallel statement, though here the picture includes man pitching in with a will. It's curious how quickly our minds rush to console ourselves with the thought that, after all, slaughterhouses are somehow exceptional places. Maybe, but meat isn't an exceptional diet. The radical antithesis of metaphysics and materialism appears in another form. Roman Catholic theologians and their spiritual fellow-travellers are apt to reassure themselves with the dogma that since animals have no souls, God isn't perplexed by the fact that men kill them to eat, whereas he would be perplexed if men had to eat men to live. Indeed if cannibalism is mythically so interesting, it's because the slide from animal to human meat is so easy that early and massive tabus are needed to block it, and the rites of the last supper derive their poignancy from evoking just that impulse, faintly, and in an ethically beautiful form. Ironically, therefore, it's not the Roman Catholic church, but Brigitte Bardot,

who cares about man's unnecessary inhumanity to animals in slaughterhouses. It's enough to make the mythical St Francis of Assissi turn in his grave, though the historical St Francis was pretty callous himself. Not that Franju's holy rage at the carnivorous aspects of existence is meant to make us vegetarians, still less to paralyse us with guilt. Rather, it's a reminder that what is inevitable may also be spiritually unendurable, that what is justifiable may be atrocious, that the best we can do will always be an organized butchery – and the possible best is itself light-years from fulfilment. Only when we have realised that, like our Mad Mother Nature, our Mad Father Society is an organization of deaths as well as of lives, can we become more aware, gentle, alive, sad, free for a Schweitzerian reverence for life, i.e. a reverence for all lives, and not just the next one. The road to spiritual maturity leads, not upwards into the clouds, but downwards, into a relentless materialism.

Whether to develop or refute it, scarcely a critic has ever resisted the comparison between Franju's **Le Sang Des Bêtes** and Resnais' **Nuit Et Brouillard**, that is, between the slaughterhouses for animals and the slaughterhouses for men. The town-hall clock strikes twelve as a craftsman hacks, that hacking becomes the city centre; the church spires nestle prettily in the green countryside round Buchenwald. A butcher sings *La Mer*, camp orchestras strike up marches from musical comedy. Above all, the tone is reminiscent: the tenderness, the finesse, the avoidance of easy indignation.

Photograph: Dennis Morris

sex pistols: "god save the queen"

An unadorned performance video, filmed by Julien Temple, showing the Sex Pistols miming to their most inflammatory anthem, **God Save The Queen** was shot back to back (at the old Marquee club in Soho, in 1977) with the very similar promo for "Pretty Vacant"; between them, the two films capture the pure essence of rock and roll and youth rebellion. More than that though, **God Save The Queen** is the crystallization of a historic moment in time, a moment when establishment England was reeling beneath the musical and political onslaught of punk rock, masterminded by Malcolm McLaren and executed by the Pistols. Although the song was top of the hit parade, the BBC were in denial and refused to even acknowledge its existence; therefore, effectively banned for "treason", neither the video nor the track itself was ever aired. Temple's video clearly shows why – fear. A perfect temporal/spatial fusion of image, words, attitude, noise, power, aggression, energy, and revolutionary *zeitgeist*, **God Save The Queen** was the most vital and significant rock film since the convulsive satanic beauty of the Stones' **Jumping Jack Flash**.

tokyo 1969: revolutionary image-thieves in the disintegrating city

Tokyo's period of urban unrest extended across the 1960s, beginning with widespread rioting, and demonstrations around the parliament building, in 1960, and culminating in sustained protests and confrontations that lasted throughout 1968 and 1969, before mutating into other forms; film constituted a sensitised medium for the exploration of that uproar, with a number of directors initiating stylistic experiments and outstanding approaches to the representation of urban space in transformation. In particular, two films from 1969, Toshio Matsumoto's **Funeral Parade Of Roses (Bara No Soretsu)** and Nagisa Oshima's **Diary Of A Shinjuku Thief (Shinjuku Dorobō Nikki)**, probed the intimate rapport between the dynamics of Tokyo's urban unrest and the intensive artistic and sexual experimentation ongoing during that period in the city's Shinjuku district. This essay gives an account of the unique cultural history of postwar Tokyo, and its relationship to filmmaking; it then examines the particular challenges faced by filmmakers in creating images of the excessive space of Tokyo, looking in particular at sequences in films by Chris Marker and Andrei Tarkovsky. The essay then considers **Funeral Parade Of Roses** and **Diary Of A Shinjuku Thief** as exceptional filmic explorations of the urban culture of Tokyo (a culture viewed by many of its participants as a revolutionary one); it then concludes by evaluating the enduring relevance of that strand of urban filmmaking for contemporary Tokyo's visual culture.

Urban filmmaking in Tokyo at the end of the 1960s reflects the very particular dynamics and range of filmmaking practice during that era, as well as the wide-ranging architectural expansion and experimentation that had been taking place in the city during the preceding decade. In the face of a studio system which appeared to be increasingly disintegrating, Tokyo-based filmmakers operated in a vast range and combination of forms and styles, from the structuralist experimental filmmaking exemplified by Takahiko Iimura, to independently or collaboratively funded projects, often preoccupied with issues of sexuality and dissident political issues, as in the films of Shuji Terayama. Filmmakers often oscillated between working on studio-funded projects and more independent projects, at a time when the hard-pressed studios were focusing their attention on previously peripheral genres, such as pornographic and horror films, often commissioning directors to work on entire series of such films. To some extent, this flexibility and mutability of late-1960s filmmaking in Tokyo replicates that of European filmmaking of the same period, including its concerns with political and sexual issues and with stylistic experimentation; however, the particular historical and cultural context of Japan in the late 1960s, and its influence on urban life and on urban representations in film, is distinctly different from that of Europe.

Both the visual form of Tokyo as an urban entity, and the tensions which generated the exceptional filmmaking of the late 1960s, have their origins in the large-scale destruction of the city during the Second World War, and the Occupation by US military forces which succeeded that destruction. As with many other industrial cities in Japan, Tokyo was extensively fire-bombed, especially in March 1945, with enormous casualties in the urban population; entire areas of the city vanished, and four million people fled the city in the war's closing months. As well as the human losses, the firebombing also engulfed Tokyo's libraries, film-archives, and historical buildings such as temples and shrines, so that much of the city's historical and cultural history became erased. The American film-historian and filmmaker, Donald Richie, arrived in the city in the following year, 1946, and commented on the visual reconfiguration of the city which its destruction had generated: 'I stand at the main

crossing on the Ginza, nothing between me and the mountain [Mount Fuji] ... I stand and watch the mountain fade. From this crossing it had not been seen since Edo times, but now all the buildings between are cinders. Between me and Fuji is a burned wasteland, a vast and blackened plain where a city had once stood.'(1)

For many young filmmakers, artists and architects in Tokyo, such as Arata Isozaki and Juro Kara (the theatre-director who plays one of the central characters in **Diary Of A Shinjuku Thief**), the erasure of the city also entailed the sweeping-away of the constrictive militarist and familial structures of the pre-war era, so the city's destruction also possessed an exhilarating aspect, with the sense that the city could now be transformed from scratch into an entirely new entity. However, the US Occupation of Japan, which extended from 1945 to 1952, created its own unprecedented cultural impact, including that upon cinema, since the American authorities imposed an often idiosyncratic censorship regime on Japanese filmmaking. American military forces remained in Japan, and during the era of the Vietnam war, air-bases close to Tokyo were to be used extensively to supply and reinforce the US war-effort. However, the most significant legacy of the US Occupation was the imposition upon Japan of a long-term treaty which many Japanese citizens, students and filmmakers, saw as subjugating the country to both the military and cultural power of the USA. The treaty, known as the 'Treaty of Mutual Cooperation and Security between the United States and Japan', needed to be ratified once a decade after its initial signature in 1960, and the violent urban-protests and street-battles – which form the key narrative event that frames late-1960s films such as **Funeral Parade Of Roses** and **Diary Of A Shinjuku Thief** – were related in part to the treaty's imminent renewal.

Those two films, then, are impelled by a very specific set of cultural and historical traumas, which impact directly upon the urban space of Tokyo as the location for the fast-moving riots and protests which inflect the films' narratives. Urban space is in a multiple state of turmoil in such films, and therefore needs to be captured in a mobile way which accentuates the ongoing process of urban and human mutation taking place; filmmakers such as Matsumoto and Oshima responded to those imperatives by adopting styles of filmmaking such as extensive use of handheld cameras and blurred or manipulated images, to indicate the speed with which the city's uproar is being perceived.

In many ways, the process of filming the urban space of Tokyo presents very distinctive challenges and imperatives for filmmakers. The city has often been perceived, especially by visitors, as an excessive urban space, impossible to grasp in its entirety, labyrinthine in structure, extending into limitless suburban sprawl. Those

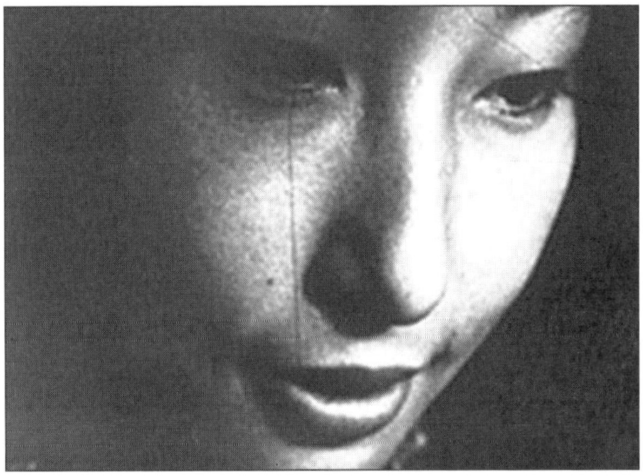

demands of the city upon its filmmakers are present in works such as those of Matsumoto and Oshima, and the turmoil of the period of fast-moving street-protests, at the end of the 1960s, served only to exacerbate that aura of excess. But the urban gestures and movements of Tokyo have also been revealingly seized by filmmakers from other countries, who have often incorporated fragments from the engulfing space of the megalopolis into films which are composed of trajectories across the city, generated in order to probe issues of memory and representation. From this perspective, Tokyo requires images which approach it at a tangent, either those resulting from a distinctive style of urban filmmaking, or those which disregard the archetypal images of a city of packed crowds, image-screens and multi-storey corporate towers, and seek to reinvent or realign urban space, in a parallel way to that in which the street-protestors of the late 1960s aimed to do.

The French filmmaker and traveller, Chris Marker, visited Tokyo over a period of time that spans the city's seminal filmic moment of 1969. Marker arrived in Tokyo with the plan to film the Olympic Games of 1964, the preparations for which entailed a wide-ranging transformation of urban space, including the construction of many inner-city highways, often poised one on top of the other in the city's most crowded areas. During that visit, Marker made the film **The Koumiko Mystery**, about his obsession with a young Japanese woman. But the most revealing of Marker's Tokyo images were collected in his film **Sunless** (**Sans Soleil**), from 1982, in which Marker returns to the city after a long absence, and films the locations of the city in which his memory has concentrated past moments – with those moments represented by past film-images, so that film itself supplants the city. Marker visits sites with individual resonances for him, such as the Gotokuji temple, dedicated to the cats of Tokyo, but also amasses his images on the move, in transit from site to site, and from moment to moment, filming the sleeping inhabitants of subway trains, and interposing the hallucinations and nightmares – drawn from Japanese popular culture and television shows – which occupy their mental space. In his commentary, Marker evokes Tokyo's unique urban space: 'Tokyo is a city criss-crossed by trains, tied together with electric wire, she shows her veins ... One could get lost in the great architectural masses and the accumulation of details, and that created the cheapest images of Tokyo: overcrowded, megalomaniacal, inhuman. He thought he saw more subtle cycles there, rhythms, clusters of faces caught sight of in passing, as different and precise as groups of instruments.' Marker also filmed confrontations between protesters and riot-police, just as Matsumoto and Oshima had done, though Marker's images are primarily those of protests about the construction of the Narita airport in the countryside outside Tokyo, which involved the uprooting of numerous farming communities. He includes images of those violent riots in the

 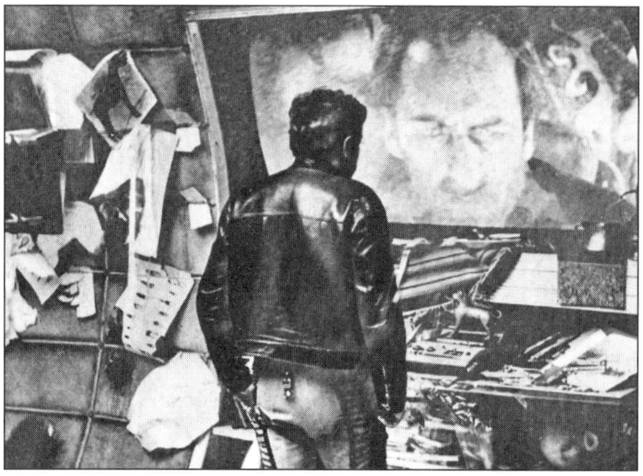

computer-treated sequences of **Sunless**, as images which have entered the area which he calls the 'Zone': an area, inspired by Tarkovsky's film **Stalker**, that propels the human eye beyond the habitual parameters of both the filmic and the urban, into an amalgam of future technologies and endless spatial mutations.

Andrei Tarkovsky himself visited Tokyo during September 1971, at a time when the urban protest-movement of two or three years earlier had itself mutated, with many of its young participants despairing of the possibility of radical or revolutionary social change, and entering a kind of 'internal exile' within the ascendant corporate Japan of the 1970s, while others, inspired by terrorist movements in Europe, joined Japan's own terrorist groups, notably the Japanese Red Army, the 'Sekigun-ha', founded in 1971 and allied to the Popular Movement for the Liberation of Palestine. Tarkovsky perceived Tokyo as a salutary urban space, writing in his diary: 'Japan is a wonderful country, of course. Nothing in common with Europe or America. Tokyo is an amazing city. There's not a single factory chimney, not a single house that looks like any other.'(2) In this sense, Tarkovsky's perception of Tokyo's urban space is at profound variance with many other visitors to the city, who saw it as a site enduringly imprinted with the residues of its US Occupation, and also noted an extreme homogeneity in its architectural forms, especially those of its suburbs. Tarkovsky effectively streamlines and reconfigures the city for his filmic purposes. He had arrived in Tokyo to shoot a sequence for his film **Solaris**, in which an astronaut, Berton, is inhabiting what Tarkovsky calls 'a town of the future': an unnamed megalopolis entirely composed of highway underpasses and overpasses, bordered by immense towers. Berton has an argument with another astronaut, Kelvin, who is shortly to leave on a mission to the planet Solaris; Berton then abruptly leaves Kelvin's rural house, and in an extended five-minute sequence, the astronaut drives through the urban terrain of Tokyo at speed, from underpass to overpass, through the dense network of highways which had been constructed in advance of the 1964 Olympic Games. Finally, the camera ascends, away from Berton's car, in order to view the chaos of intersecting highway-junctions from above. Once the sequence is over, Tokyo, which has never been identified, vanishes from the film. The city may be reinvented by such fragmentary apparitions within the films of visitors to Tokyo, such as Marker and Tarkovsky, in which memory, imagination and duration are intensively probed by transits across the face of the city, using the film-camera to examine urban facades and to unleash sensations. But in films actually centred within the axis of Tokyo's unrest of the late-1960s, as with **Funeral Parade Of Roses** and **Diary Of A Shinjuku Thief**, that charge of urban tension comes to generate very distinctive stylistic forms of urban filmmaking.

Matsumoto's film **Funeral Parade Of Roses** was principally shot on the streets of Tokyo, notably in the district of Shinjuku, which in the late 1960s was intimately associated with experiments in visual arts, as the location of nightclubs for the city's gay cultures, and especially as the axis for the mass street-protests which took place throughout 1968 and 1969. One area, in particular, a large plaza alongside the area's railway station, was seen as a gathering place for both demonstrators and for sexual outcasts; it also formed an impromptu space for spectacles by performance artists, and also comprises the key location for Oshima's **Diary Of A Shinjuku Thief**. The department stores and business towers surrounding the plaza were already illuminated with immense neon hoardings advertising technology corporations, and by the end of the following decade, those hoardings had been replaced by the moving-image screens which reputedly inspired Ridley Scott, in planning his film **Blade Runner** (1982), for the depiction of an urban amalgam that oscillates between Los Angeles and Tokyo. The Shinjuku district had a heavy police presence, and Matsumoto was unable to obtain official permission to film there. As a result, the exterior sequences of the film were done covertly, usually in one take, before the police arrived to break up the filmmaking process. This urgency and spontaneity in part determines the stylistic form of **Funeral Parade Of Roses**, as it does with **Diary Of A Shinjuku Thief**, shot in similar conditions of rapidity. The film image becomes one infused with a sense of immediacy, with urban space caught by hand-held cameras in single takes, which focus primarily on the faces and bodies of the characters in their juxtaposition with the surrounding buildings' facades; such approaches resonate from the strategies of neo-realist filmmaking in Europe. The film's interior spaces form similarly improvised ones, shot in small rooms, often crowded with figures dancing or undertaking sexual acts, so that the camera has to manoeuvre and negotiate its way through space, with a perpetual sense of mobility.

That element of flexibility also relates to the particular forms of filmmaking adopted by young directors such as Matsumoto and Oshima in late 1960s Tokyo, and to the ways in which their films were financed and distributed. Filmmakers could form alliances with the studio-system, and adapt their preoccupations to the demands of the studios' prevalent genres of the time, such as youth-culture, pornographic, and horror films. At the same time, several collective organisations of independent film-production existed in Tokyo, as they did at that time in European countries such as Germany, and both **Funeral Parade Of Roses** and **Diary Of A Shinjuku Thief** were produced by the Art Theatre Guild company, which had been formed in 1961 and also produced films by Shuji

Terayama. Although such production structures possessed relatively small budgets, they were associated with networks of autonomous cinemas which allowed the films to be widely seen. Both independent and studio-based filmmaking of the time presented combinations of flexibility and constriction, either in terms of the funds available for filmmaking, or the stylistic parameters of filmmaking. **Funeral Parade Of Roses** was Matsumoto's first feature film, and rather than moving subsequently into studio productions, his later work extended further into experimental forms, in short films which analysed issues of camera movement and the manipulation or multiplication of visual images.

The narrative of **Funeral Parade Of Roses**, drawn obliquely from Greek mythology, concerns a young transvestite named Eddie who has previously murdered his mother and now works as a prostitute in a gay bar in Shinjuku, the Bar Genet. He also pursues friendships with other transvestites and with a group of young revolutionaries who are preoccupied with the ongoing street-riots. Eddie has an affair with the bar's drug-dealing proprietor, but when the proprietor discovers that he is actually Eddie's father, he stabs himself to death in their apartment, leading Eddie to then pierce his own eyes with the same knife, before going out onto the street, still clutching the knife, and attracting a crowd of onlookers; the final shot of the film circles through those onlookers before focusing on the knife, poised against the face of the city.

Funeral Parade Of Roses is located in the gay sub-cultures of Tokyo, which literally take place underground, below street-level, especially in bars, night-clubs and art-galleries, as well as on the urban surfaces. In many of the subterranean, interior sequences of the film, dense crowds of figures amass, so that the film-camera must infiltrate its way between the human figures. Similarly, once the action shifts to street-level, the camera follows the film's characters through enclosing masses of figures, who often obstruct or assault those characters. The filming of Tokyo's urban space demands a sense of mobility that remains adhered to the bodies of the protagonists, as they attempt to penetrate that space. The opening-out of urban space only emerges when the camera ascends to a viewing-position above the city, in the same way that Tarkovsky, in the final image of his Tokyo sequence in Solaris, films the highway junctions of Tokyo as a panorama, from above. In **Funeral Parade Of Roses**, those openings of urban space, from density to expansion, are situated at moments when the camera either looks down on the plazas of Shinjuku, from the summits of adjacent buildings, or else when the characters ascend to the viewing platform of a tower which gives a perspective of the entire city.

In **Funeral Parade Of Roses**, the urban space of Tokyo is seen by its characters as being involved in a

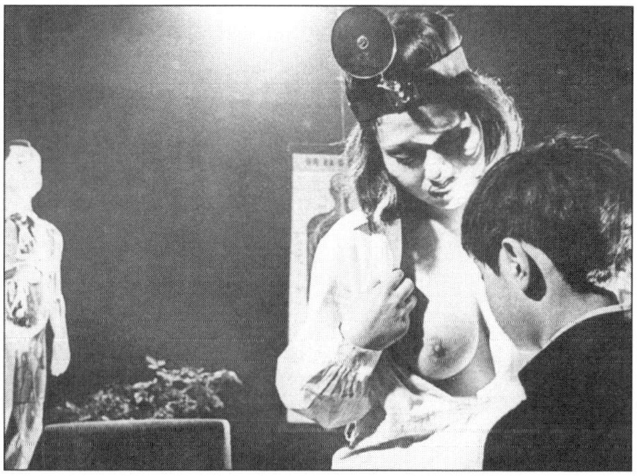

process of disintegration, reflecting the widespread perception of the time in Japan that rapid urban proliferation, together with pollution and the exhausting of natural resources, had radically destabilised the environment of the country, whose precarious existence was also mediated by the culture of violent protest against the country's presence of US military power. Urban space constantly fragments in the film. In one of its sequences, the funeral takes place of the manager of the Bar Genet, who has committed suicide out of jealousy about the relationship between Eddie and the bar's proprietor. After the funeral has ended, Eddie notices that much of the vast, decrepit cemetery has become waterlogged, and that many tombs have subsided, vanishing below the water. That disintegration of the cemetery is explicitly that of Tokyo itself, and Eddie exclaims that he wishes that not only Tokyo, but the entirety of Japan, would sink below water and disappear. The city is moving in precarious transits between moments of past disappearance, such as that of its destruction by firebombing in 1945, to future moments in which its excess, or the violence generated by its protest movements, may also entail the vanishing from sight of its space.

The title of a film directed by Shuji Terayama in the same era incites its spectators: **Throw Away Your Books, Let's Go Out Into The Streets**. However, the young revolutionaries of **Funeral Parade Of Roses** are never seen in the streets of Tokyo, and decline to participate in the demonstrations taking place at the moment in which the film is set. Instead, in company with Eddie, they remain enclosed in interior spaces, engaged in wild sex parties, and watching the television news broadcasts which show images of the ongoing confrontations between young protesters and riot-police. They also make films of the television news images, and then project those films, of the media images of riots, to themselves, in the same room, with the film-images distorted by technological processes of replication, in a parallel way to those which Chris Marker includes as the contents of the 'Zone', in his film **Sunless**. Matsumoto anticipates a global obsession with media images of conflict, and the loss of a direct physical contact with urban protest. Revolution has been abstracted, and transformed into ever-diminishing media images, which form a source of excitation, for sexual acts or for the filmmaking process itself, but not for social activism.

Matsumoto also demonstrates the estrangement and familiarisation of urban space through film, by including a number of interview sequences in **Funeral Parade Of Roses**, clearly resonant of those in films by Jean-Luc Godard, and which insurge into the film, as documentary elements, to intentionally fracture its linear narrative consistency. In those sequences, Matsumoto conducts dialogues with young transvestites in the avenues of Shinjuku,

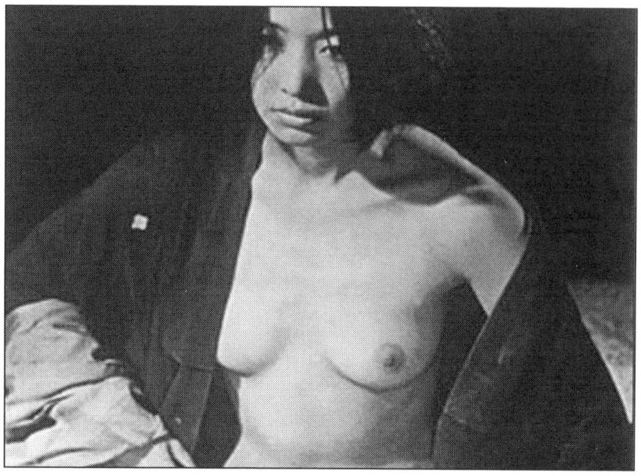

filming them at night against the background of the district's illuminated buildings. Most of the interview sequences follow a set framework, in which the same questions are posed and the same answers are given, so that they form a repetitive element of the film, providing a sense of stability within the disintegration and furore which the narrative itself carries. In part, that stability is provided by the recognisable urban presence, of the familiar plazas and hoardings of the Shinjuku district. The city may be eroding and submerging into riots, and the film's characters are all heading into death, but the distinctive urban aura of Shinjuku allows momentary coherings of filmic space.

Oshima's film **Diary Of A Shinjuku Thief**, filmed around the same period as **Funeral Parade Of Roses**, opens with a sequence set in the same Tokyo location: the plaza alongside the Shinjuku railway station, where a theatre company are staging an open-air performance. In fact, the film never leaves the Shinjuku district, focusing on a narrow psychogeographical area which the film relates to the interior journey of its central character, Birdey, a young book-thief who steals books from the shelves at the huge Kinokuniya bookshop, located directly alongside the Shinjuku plaza. In many ways, the film attempts to generate a narrative element from the particular resonances of that urban location, and its reputation as a site for counter-cultures and sexual experimentation, in the way that filmmakers of the same era might have selected as locations the Haight-Ashbury district of San Francisco, or the Kreuzberg district of West Berlin, in order to conjure a parallel aura of urban exploration. Oshima's film is concerned more explicitly than **Funeral Parade Of Roses** with making connections between sexual acts and revolution, cutting directly between sex-scenes and shots of the street-riots in Shinjuku; the film ends with an extended sequence of rioting, so that its narrative is one that is left open, as though prised-apart by the engulfing violent uproar of the period.

However, one factor which unites the two films is their obsession with the work of the French writer Jean Genet, whose novels are cited in both films' titles, and whose film **Un Chant d'Amour**, from 1950, had been distributed internationally via filmmakers' co-operatives and seen by directors in Japan; it exerts a strong stylistic influence on the filming of sexual acts in **Funeral Parade Of Roses**. The naming of the nightclub where Eddie works in that film forms a homage to Genet, and when Birdie steals books from the Kinokuniya bookshop, he heads directly for the works of Genet, who had himself been a book-thief and was imprisoned several times for those thefts. Genet was at the height of his international reputation in 1969, engaged in that period in his support for the Palestinians, for the Black Panther movement in the USA, and for the rights of immigrant workers in France

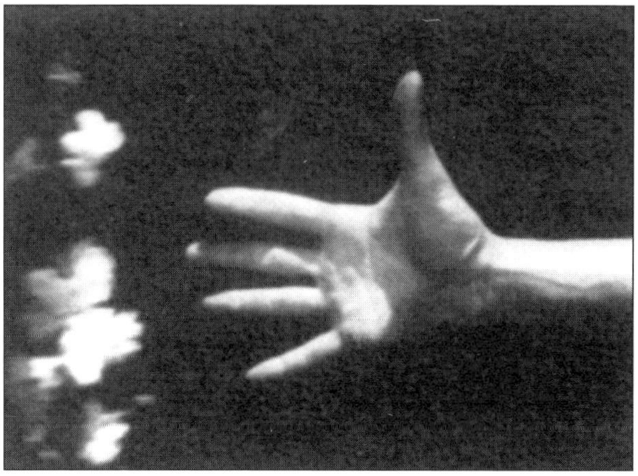

itself; all of his novels had been translated into Japanese, and he was a seminal figure for many of Tokyo's experimental filmmakers, artists, choreographers and theatre directors, as he remains in contemporary Tokyo. By an aberrant urban coincidence, Genet spent part of 1969 in Tokyo, where he visited his friend Jackie Maglia, and took part in several of the largest and most violent of the confrontations between the student movements and riot-police, in November and December of that year. Maglia recalled Genet's participation in the demonstrations: 'People hooked up to one another ... so they'd be harder to arrest. Genet pretended to be "reviewing" the masked soldiers who'd come to control the crowd. He looked each soldier squarely in the eye (many of them were handsome).'(3) However, Genet declined to meet filmmakers and artists while in Tokyo.

Even more than Matsumoto's film, **Diary Of A Shinjuku Thief** is a film of urban fragments, in which narrative elements are disconnected and subordinated to the exploration of urban space. The film comprises a set of momentary encounters, transits and pursuits, between the book-thief and a female assistant at the Kinokuniya bookshop who arrests him in the act of theft, and between them and a theatre director played by Juro Kara. As with **Funeral Parade Of Roses**, the film focuses on the ability of the mobile camera to scan the surfaces and subterraneas of the city, and collect traces and residues, including those imprinted upon exterior walls and buildings in the forms of graffiti and advertising hoardings, which then amass, to form a representation of the city, in many ways allied to those created by neo-realist works, as one in a state of crisis. Although the exploration of urban space is largely accorded the work of defining and carrying the film – to the point at which, in **Diary Of A Shinjuku Thief**, the characters occasionally appear peripheral to the film's preoccupations – that urban space is itself one which is seen as disintegrating, subject to perpetual amendment, and presented as a sequence of fragments which will never cohere.

In both **Funeral Parade Of Roses** and **Diary Of A Shinjuku Thief**, the revolutionary aspirations of the protesters are treated by the filmmakers with a degree of irony, and linked to the ideas of revolution as an art of performance which Genet had developed in his theatrical work. The revolutionary 'cell' in Matsumoto's film never leave their room, and become consumed by the media images of the riots taking place in the avenues outside; the sexual imperatives around the relationship between the two characters in **Diary Of A Shinjuku Thief** also render them largely oblivious to the riots which finally engulf the entire film. This preoccupation with an oblique, ambivalent relationship to activism and revolutionary commitment is also present in films by the director Koji Wakamatsu, who analysed the rapport between sexual and revolutionary acts in his films of the same era,

 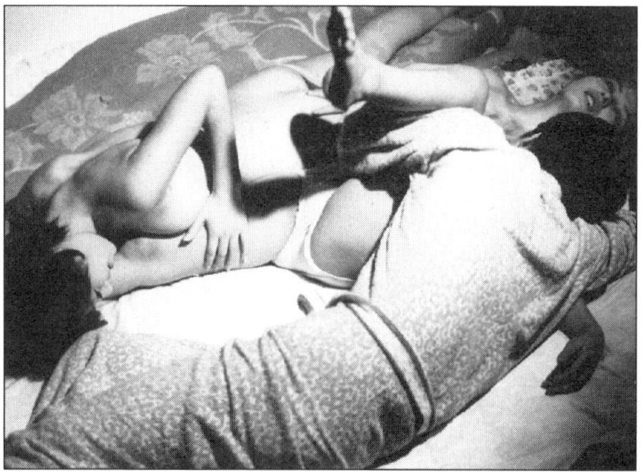

structured in the form of exploitation or pornographic films. Wakamatsu was also preoccupied with the connections between the protest-culture of late-1960s Tokyo and the terrorist movements which emerged, directly or indirectly, from that culture; he visited the Palestinian liberation movements in 1971, and recently made a new film, **United Red Army** (2008), which looks back at the terrorist groups of 1970s Japan and at their implosive internal dynamics. Both **Funeral Parade Of Roses** and **Diary Of A Shinjuku Thief** appear prescient of the aftermath of the urban riots in late-1960s Tokyo, in their depictions both of an all-consuming apathy, and of forms of terrorism whose imageries and definitions could be endlessly manipulated and distorted.

In that same period, the Tokyo-based filmmaker Donald Richie made his film **Cybele**, which, like **Funeral Parade Of Roses**, adopts a mythic narrative structure and uses a cemetery location, that of the vast Yanaka cemetery in eastern Tokyo, to explore its concern with urban and cultural disintegration. In the final sequence of his film, Richie depicted a group of naked figures who appeared to have been slaughtered and piled-up on top of each other – images which led to the censorship and banning of the film in numerous countries. In some ways, those images intimate an overturning of the sense of exhilaration and often-playful experimentation which had occupied Tokyo-based filmmakers during the second half of the 1960s, and resonate instead, even against the filmmaker's intentions, more directly from wartime images such as those of the results of the US firebombing of the city in 1945. Those unexpected transits across time, in Japanese cinema of the late 1960s, are as revealing as the perpetual movements through urban space which propelled those films' narratives and determined their distinctive stylistic texture.

The images of Tokyo's urban space, in a state of violent turmoil, remain resonant ones for filmmaking and for digital arts in contemporary Tokyo, evident, for example, in the work of the director Shinya Tsukamoto and the mutating megalopolis of his films, such as **Tokyo Fist**. The films of Takashi Miike carry an allied preoccupation, to those of **Funeral Parade Of Roses** and **Diary Of A Shinjuku Thief**, with the city's Shinjuku district as a unique urban environment in which events habitually occur that would otherwise be impossible and unconceivable, and which need to be seized at speed. The particular ethos of late-1960s film-production and distribution structures in Japan, exemplified by the Art Theatre Guild, still survives in Tokyo through institutions such as Image Forum. After being rarely seen for many years, **Funeral Parade Of Roses** and **Diary Of A Shinjuku Thief** were, in many ways, resuscitated by the DVD medium, which allowed viewers the opportunity to reconstruct the time and space of their fast-moving urban transits. Even though the urban space of Tokyo, including that of

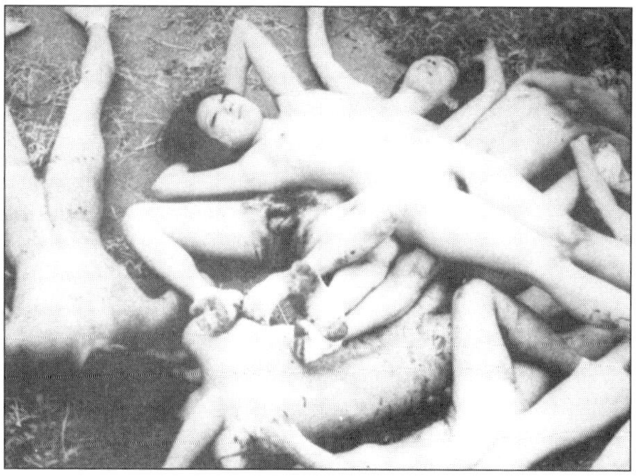

Shinjuku, is now largely unrecognisable from its late-1960s documentation in films such as those by Matsumoto and Oshima, it still presents an open environment for filmmakers and digital artists preoccupied with the scanning of urban mutations, and with the exploration of pivotal moments of disquiet and unease with the forms of the city.

That filmic exploration often took the form of an intimate examination of urban surfaces, and their interaction with the human figures poised against them. The urban surfaces of Tokyo, at the end of the 1960s, mediated a set of traces and indicators, about memory and conflict and sexual dynamics, that appeared precarious and unstable, and had to be recorded with both urgency and flexibility, in movements across the face of the city, generating films which enduringly appear as vital archives, of the forms of urban space in a state of uproar and transformation.

Notes

1. Donald Riche, *Tokyo: A View of the City* (Reaktion Books, London and Washington DC, 1999), p.27.
2. Andrei Tarkovsky, *Time Within Time: The Diaries 1970-1986* (Faber and Faber, London, 1994), pp.43-44.
3. Edmund White, *Genet* (Chatto and Windus, London, 1993), p.596.

"las hurdes": the commentary

The following text represents the first-ever full and accurate translation of Luis Buñuel's commentary for his subversive documentary *Las Hurdes* (1932):

This film essay on human geography was shot in 1932 – shortly after the Spanish Republic came into being.

The region you are going to visit, Las Hurdes, has been viewed by geographers and travellers as a barren and inhospitable one, whose population struggle ceaselessly to survive.

Until the first road was built there, in 1922, Las Hurdes was almost unknown, both to the world and even to the Spanish.

Across Europe, there exist primitive, uncivilized regions. Las Hurdes is situated only one hundred kilometres from

Salamanca, one of Spain's centres of high culture.

The region is difficult to reach, isolated by high mountains that are covered with briars and laudanum-shrubs.

Before reaching Las Hurdes, we must travel via La Alberca – a wealthy and feudal village, with a great influence on the life of Las Hurdes, most of whose inhabitants are dependent upon it.

Here is the church of La Alberca. Two death's heads in niches seem to rule over the village's fate.

The houses are mostly on three levels, with an architecture rare in Spain. They give the streets an appearance of the Middle Ages.

Most houses have, engraved above the door, a religious inscription: HAIL MARY, THE IMMACULATE, WHO CONCEIVED WITHOUT SIN.

On the day of our arrival, we see the village's women arranging their hair, and wearing their best clothes. We ask what they are getting themselves ready for.

They reply that we must go to the church square, where a strange and savage ritual is about to be celebrated, as in every year.

In front of the assembled population, the most recently married men – in 1932, at the time of our journey, they were the six you see here – must each rip off a cock's head.

A rope is stretched between two street corners, with a cock attached to it by the feet.

Each rider must gallop up, to rip off the head of a cock.

The scene is cruel.

But our duty of objectivity compels us to show it to you.

As you see, the rider's skill doesn't lessen the act's cruelty. If a rider fails, he turns around and tries again, as many times as necessary – but each man must rip off a head.

This ritual of blood certainly hides complex sexual symbols.

But we are not going to analyse them now.

After the newly-married men have paraded the cocks' heads in triumph, through every square and street, they distribute wine to the entire population. The cupbearers also give thousands of wafers to the village's inhabitants.

In the crowd, we spot a child, richly adorned with medallions of silver. Christian images appear on these medallions, but we can't resist thinking of the amulets of the primitive peoples of Africa and Oceania.

At seven in the evening, we leave behind La Alberca, where nearly everyone is already drunk, and head up into the mountains. After only three kilometres, the panorama of Las Hurdes is already revealed.

Here are the criss-crossed mountains – at the heart of which are spread out the fifty-two villages, with a combined population of 8,000, which make up Las Hurdes.

We have to descend a steep slope, then cross the splendid valley of Las Batuecas, currently inhabited by an old monk who lives there surrounded by servants.

Carmelite monks lived in this valley for four centuries, preaching Christianity in the largest villages of Las Hurdes.

Now, the monastery is deserted apart from the few people we mentioned.

There remain only ruins, surrounded by a landscape of wild, grandiose beauty.

Traces of vibrant prehistoric life survive in Las Batuecas. In prehistoric caves, you find skilfully executed paintings, showing men, goats, and bees.

Toads, grass-snakes and lizards are these ruins' current inhabitants.

The vegetation is especially rich – more than two hundred kinds of trees grow freely here. But, only five kilometres from this valley, the soil suddenly changes – apart from a few fruit trees, there is nothing but shrubs and briar.

A wall, eight kilometres in circumference, surrounds the monastery, protecting it from attack by the area's many wolves and wild boar. Within the area of safety created by the wall, the ruins of several hermitages are spread out here and there, each marked by one or more cypresses.

At the time when the monastery was inhabited, the anchorites had to peal their hermitages' bells every night at midnight. The monastery's prior then responded with his great bell.

Behind these peaks – which still belong to Las Batuecas – begins Las Hurdes.

After crossing them, we are now in the landscape of Las Hurdes.

This village, Aceitunilla, is situated in one of the poorest valleys.

The white building is the recently built school. In the streets along the mountain side, we observe the inhabitants'

daily life. A strange detail is that, in all the villages of Las Hurdes, we never heard any singing.

In the middle of the village, you occasionally see a wretched little stream, running down from the mountain. In summer, it's the only water the village has. The villagers use it, despite its disgusting state of filth.

Here are a few scenes shot as we walked around. The stream is used for everything. Here, three little girls are eating bread soaked in the water. Bread: which, until very recently, was almost unknown in Las Hurdes. This bread is given to the girls by the schoolmaster, who usually forces the children to eat the bread in his presence, fearing that if the children take it home, their parents will immediately steal it.

The children are called into school.

These ragged, barefoot children receive the same education as that given to children in primary schools worldwide.

Their clothes are brought here by those inhabitants of Las Hurdes who migrate for several months each year to the regions of Castile and Andalusia.

They specialize there in begging.

When they return, they divide out the clothes in exchange for potatoes. The clothes are usually so patched-together that there hardly remains a piece of the original material.

These starving children learn – like children everywhere – that the sum of a triangle's angles is equal to two right-angles.

In several villages of Las Hurdes, and especially here in Aceitunilla, most children are 'Pilus': that is, abandoned children, whom the women of Las Hurdes collect from the Public Assistance Center in Ciudad Rodrigo, two days' walk away through the mountains. The women agree to raise them in return for fifteen pesetas each month.

This miserable sum was used to support an entire family – until the day, still recent, when the 'Pilus industry' was outlawed here.

We discover an unexpected, shocking image. Isn't it outrageous for such a picture to be here?

At random, we open up a book of morals which we find on a table. At our request, one of the brightest children inscribes a maxim from the book, on the blackboard. The morality taught to these children is identical to that which rules our civilized work: RESPECT OTHER PEOPLE'S PROPERTY.

In this comparatively rich valley, we see a few walnut, olive and cherry trees.

This is the village of Martinandran. These scab-shapes you can see between the trees evoke the carapace of some fabulous animal. In fact, they're the houses' roofs.

When we enter the village, a choir of coughing welcomes us in.

Most people here are ill.

It's a spectacle of utter misery.

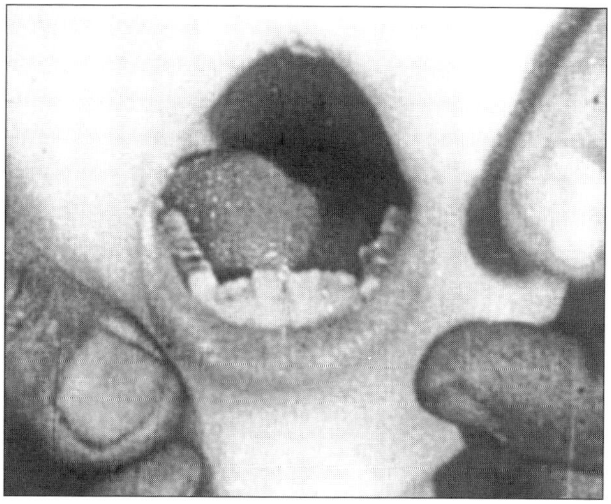

Goitre is the main illness of the Upper Hurdes – the area which will be our report's main focus. Take a look at this woman with her goitre: she's only thirty-two years old.

We visit Martinandran, accompanied by its mayor. We encounter a little girl in a deserted street. We ask the mayor what's wrong with her. He replies that she hasn't moved for three days. The child keeps complaining, so she must be sick – but we can't find out what illness she has. One of our filmcrew takes on a doctor's role. He goes up to her to find out why her throat is painful.

He asks the child to open her mouth – and we see that her gums and throat are inflamed.

Unfortunately, we can do nothing for her.

Two days later, we return to this village, and ask about the little girl.

We are told she is dead.

What do this barren land's inhabitants eat? The only, or almost the only, foods they have are potatoes and haricot beans. Even those basics are sometimes lacking each June and July.

The only meat they have is pork. Only families that are rich, if you can call them that, have a pig. Once a year, the pig is killed – and its meat devoured over 3 days.

Olive trees grow in the region's most fertile locations. Often, insects destroy the fruit.

The goat is the animal that thrives best in this arid region. Goat-milk is reserved for the seriously ill. The milk is soaked in bread – which beggars bring back from their travels and which is also set aside for the sick.

Goat-meat is only eaten when a goat meets its end. This sometimes happens, on sheer terrain with steep pathways.

Bee-keeping is the main food-industry in Las Hurdes. But the hives mostly don't belong to the people here, and even worse, the honey, extracted by the bees from heather, is very bitter.

People from La Alberca own the hives. They only leave the hives in Las Hurdes during the winter, because the weather here is milder than in the adjacent province of Salamanca. In springtime, the hives are transported to Castile. It's a frequent sight then to see one or more animals loaded with hives, heading for Castile.

One day, we encountered this donkey with its load of hives, which two people from Las Hurdes were leading towards Salamanca.

A little later, while we were having a quiet meal, we heard cries for help.

A hive had fallen from the tethered animal, which the bees were now attacking.

The donkey's frenetic movements of self-defence led to the other hives falling, too – and swarms of bees engulfed it.

An hour later, the animal was dead.

One month before we arrived in Las Hurdes, three men and eleven mules had died in the same way.

May and June are the hardest months for the people of Las Hurdes, whose potatoes have run out by that time.

They then eat cherries – and hunger causes them to eat unripened cherries, which provoke dysentery.

It's also the time of migration. All of the men who aren't sick or feverish set out for Castile or Extremadura to try to get harvest work.

We encounter several of these caravans of ten, thirty, or fifty men, equipped only with blankets. They have no money, no bread – and they're heading far away, on foot, to look for work.

Several days later, we meet such a group returning exactly as they left, with no money, no bread.

We've now reached one of the key moments in this report: How do the people of Las Hurdes construct a field capable of growing what they need to eat?

They start by choosing some land next to the river. Together with their wives, parents and friends, they then clear away the heather and shrubs. Their tools are basic: picks, shovels. They have nothing else to work with – ploughs are unknown in most villages of Las Hurdes. Once the ground is cleared, they build walls with stones, piled up without mortar. The walls will protect the field from winter floods.

Once the wall is built, they must go to search for fertile soil in the mountains. They fill their sacks and carry them through thorny areas, back to their field. This work takes several weeks. You can see that only a thin layer of earth covers their fields.

The harvest is good in the first year – but the soil lacks nitrogen and quickly becomes exhausted and barren.

All of their fields have the form of narrow strips of earth along the river. Often, winter floods annihilate a year's work in just a few seconds.

Here is the usual meandering form of a river in Las Hurdes, with small fields spread alongside it.

Without money, without animals, the people of Las Hurdes cannot acquire fertilizer. So they search out a substitute in the mountains – as with the family you see here.

The pathways are difficult, and shoes are a rarity.

The people of Las Hurdes employ a fertilizer which they make themselves out of the dried leaves of wild strawberry trees – which are not common in these mountains.

Once they find a good location they fill their sacks with the precious leaves – but up here, vipers are everywhere.

One of these peasants was bitten on the hand by a viper, several days ago, while collecting leaves.

The bite is almost never fatal in itself but the people of Las Hurdes infect themselves, sometimes fatally, in their attempts to treat it.

Once the leaves are gathered, the peasants return to their villages and spread the sacks' contents inside their houses. Animals and people together lay down on the leaves, which slowly rot until, several months later, they can be used as fertilizer.

This is the house of an inhabitant of Fragosa.

As soon as you enter, you walk on these leaves which are always a fixture of Las Hurdes houses.

This house's interior is characteristic. Only a very few, basic kitchen-utensils. Smoke exits the house however it can: no chimneys, no windows.

In summer, the rivers run almost dry. This is the cause of malaria transmitted by the 'anopheles' mosquito.

You could say that the entire population of Las Hurdes has malaria. This illness is currently being combated by the doctors of the region's three clinics.

The mosquito larva has to reach the water's surface to breathe.

If it positions itself there at a parallel angle, it's an 'anopheles' larva.

If it positions itself at a perpendicular angle, it's a 'culex' larva: that is, a harmless mosquito.

You find the adult 'anopheles' mosquito in every house in Las Hurdes – it positions itself at a perpendicular angle to the wall.

This is the result of a mosquito bite. This man, sitting near to his house, has an attack of fever.

We encounter many ill people in the streets. This sick woman, reclining on her balcony, is oblivious to us. Balconies of this or any other kind are rare in most villages of Las Hurdes.

Dwarves and cretins are present in great numbers in the Upper Hurdes.

Their families habitually use them as goat-herds.

Some cretins are dangerous.

They either flee from you – or else attack you by throwing rocks.

You meet them at nightfall in the mountains as they return to their villages.

We had great difficulty in filming some of the cretins.

Such a reality far surpasses the realism even of artists such as Zurbarán and Ribera.

The cretins' degeneration is mainly due to hunger, lack of hygiene, poverty, and incest.

The little one you see here is twenty-eight years old.

Here's another type of cretin: an old one.

And yet another cretin.

This cretin was almost feral and we could only film him thanks to one of our friends from Las Hurdes who joked with the cretin and kept him calm.

One day, we saw a group of people gathered at the door of a house – a child had just died. Here's the mother.

Someone's death is one of the rare events you can record in these wretched villages. Women ran in a group to the house of death.

We learned of the complications involved in transporting corpses, since most villages have no cemetery. The dead child had to be transported to the cemetery in Munomoral.

We decided to follow.

The corpse was placed in an animal-trough, and carried for several kilometres through scrubland. When the corpse is an adult's, it is bound to a ladder, and carried like that to the cemetery. This often involves a walk of several hours.

Here you see the child's corpse being ferried across a river.

This cemetery showed us that, despite the deep poverty of Las Hurdes, its people's moral and religious ideas are the same as everywhere in the world. Graves are marked with crosses and bits of wood.

The only traces of luxury we encountered in Las Hurdes were – the churches.

This church is in one of the wretchedest villages.

This is the interior of one of the most comfortable houses. You see the father, son, daughter-in-law, and two small children. Some cut-up paper on the wall and the aligned arrangement of pot-lids demonstrate a sense of decoration.

In some villages, an old woman roams the streets at night – the 'death-crier'.

She goes about ringing a bell and stops from time to time to recite a prayer.

All of the inhabitants of such a house live in the same room. But this house is a little more comfortable – it has a stable on the lower level, a kitchen and room on the upper level. Very unusually, it has a bed.

The people of Las Hurdes go to bed fully clothed in winter. Clothes are worn until they fall into shreds.

The old woman told us: 'Nothing keeps you more awake than thinking always of death. Recite an Ave Maria for the soul of...'

After two months in the land of Las Hurdes – we left.

In 1937, during the Spanish Civil War, Buñuel added a concluding coda to his film:

The poverty this film has shown you has a solution.

Already, in many regions of Spain, mountain-people, peasants and workers have successfully improved their living conditions by grouping together, helping one another, and demanding change from the authorities.

This determination for a better life had its result in the last elections, in the creation of the Popular Front government.

The military generals' rebellion, supported by Hitler and Mussolini, aimed to re-establish the land-owners' privileges and their peasants' role – but the workers and peasants of Spain will defeat Franco and his accomplices.

With the help of anti-fascists worldwide, peace and happiness will ensue from the Civil War and will erase forever the concentrations of misery which this film has shown you.

Translation: Stephen Barber

hitler's revenge film

On an austere granite wall enclosing the execution shed in which the group of plotters, led by Claus von Stauffenberg, who had attempted in July 1944 to blow Hitler's body apart, at his Wolf's Lair headquarters far to the east of Berlin, were mercilessly hanged with piano wire, an inscription had been made: 'Dictatorship 1933-1945', as though the spraycanned Nazi graffiti lauding that era had become detached from the contemporary surfaces of buildings in the impoverished districts of Marzahn and Lichtenberg, its typography and medium mutating, before aberrantly veering westwards across Berlin's time-scrambled terrain, to that former prison tool-shed close to the Plötzensee lake, and coming to rest on the shed's granite facade, in order to state a negation of that era. The lead letters of that inscription, installed in 1952 when one half of the original execution shed had been razed and the remaining part of the building was sealed with that memorial wall, carried their text of repudiation, although the corroded letters appeared almost identical to those in which Stalin's name had been inscribed, as a text of reverence, during that same era, on the wall of the Schönholz memorial's marble-faced room. A temporal delimiting and definitive closure had been conceived for dictatorship, and written in lead on the execution shed's enclosing wall, but retrospectively, after the vanishing of the GDR state on 3 October 1990, that state's power too had been officially assigned the status of a 'dictatorship', with its own systems and sites of torture, execution and surveillance, so that, as with the concrete bunker-eye beside the Friedrichstrasse station, that inscription of dictatorship was subject to contemporary Berlin's oblivious historical levelling and its equivalences between Nazism and Communism, and to abrupt reversals, as with the exterior and interior of Dietrich's bombed-out building in **A Foreign Affair**. The execution shed's interior had been deployed for the decapitation and hanging of petty chicken-thieves and bomb-site looters as well as forming the pivotal site for the execution of the Nazi regime's political opponents; prominent dissidents, such as the Czech writer Julius Fučík, had been transported from all over Europe to Berlin, as though only an act of execution staged within Berlin's urban parameters could successfully uproot that resistance. But the execution shed became renowned pre-eminently as the site of the hanging of the von Stauffenberg plotters, and of the filming of those executions.

In Hitler's fury at the plotters' bomb, which perforated and deafened the eardrum into which Dietrich whispers enticing obscenities in the faked newsreel sequence in **A Foreign Affair**, as well as shredding his clothes, he notoriously demanded that the remaining plotters (von Stauffenberg himself had already been shot, together with his closest co-conspirators, on the night following the botched assassination) be executed with piano wire, to render their deaths agonisingly protracted, and that the executions be filmed, as though Hitler, displaced from Berlin at his Wolf's Lair headquarters, were to himself be the absentee director of the resulting film, offhandedly subordinating the actual cinematography to his subordinates, under the supervision of Goebbels, and the Plötzensee execution shed (similar in construction and dimensions to one of the very first film-studios, that of Georges Méliès, in the Paris suburb of Montreuil) were to be transformed into a terminal film studio, for that purpose. The resulting film disappeared without trace after the fall of Berlin to the Russian forces, nine months after it was shot, but passed into legend. Myths or imaginary narratives invoking both its horror, and its impact upon its spectators, appeared in second- and third-hand accounts, from Soviet and American military sources: the cinematographers assigned to the task had been so appalled by the plotters' extended agony that they had filmed only the first two of the thousand or more executions, and had then abandoned the film in an abbreviated state; in defiance of that curtailed form, Goebbels had been so proud of his unique film-product that he had

screened it to an audience of SS cadets, in an improvised cinema at their barracks in the Berlin district of Lichterfelde, generating such an unbearable act of spectatorship that many of the cadets had exited the cinema, vomiting or weeping; and Hitler himself, despite having commissioned the film and being its absentee 'director', hated all images of blood or death, and had never watched it, preferring instead to view sentimental musicals and the late-1920s films starring Marlene Dietrich and Leni Riefenstahl.

In its disappearance or intentional suppression, the legendary but erased film shot in the Plötzensee execution shed – its granite-clad exterior now marked with the announcement and fixed time of dictatorship, like a cinema-hoarding declaring the title and starting-time for the screening of a film which has unaccountably vanished – takes on a strange spectatorial power, with the sparse and tenuous accounts of its existence compelling visitors to the Plötzensee site unconsciously to conjure up the film as they enter the sombre, glacial execution-room, and to imagine the horror of that film, at the same time as they visually reconstruct the event of the executions from the steel beam that spans the room just below ceiling-level, holding a line of wire nooses. The disappearance of the execution-film necessarily causes it to be relentlessly generated, again and again, and internally self-projected, by those visitors, with that imaginary charge accentuating and even exceeding the horror of the actual film (if it ever existed, outside of its horror's legend), unless the execution-room's own compelling emptiness may supersede, and thereby void, such imagined filmic images of horror.

demolition of pruitt-igoe housing projects

The Pruitt-Igoe Housing Projects in East St. Louis, designed by celebrated modernist architect Minoru Yamasaki in 1955, was intended to be a monument to functionality and new urban living. Yet only a few years later it had instead become an icon of inner city hell, its towers and communal spaces lapsed into crime, vandalism and disrepair. It stood only as a testament to bureaucratic inefficiency, systemic racism, and the failure of American public housing to solve the problem of poverty. Pruitt-Igoe was finally demolished in 1972, and the third and final dynamiting of the five-block structure, broadcast live on national television on July 15th of that year, became not only one of the most stunning visual events of 20th century America, but also one of the most symbolic. This footage of the demolition was later incorporated into Godfrey Reggio's experimental film **Koyaanisqatsi**, and soundtracked by Philip Glass.

pop avant-garde violence: wakamatsu koji's "shojo geba geba"

With the release of his first independently-produced film, **The Embryo Hunts In Secret** in 1966, Japanese director Koji Wakamatsu had sown the seed of a psychotic revolutionary cinema which would flower spectacularly over the next few years with the release of such stunning, controversial works as **Violated Angels**, **Go, Go, Second Time Virgin**, and **Shojo Geba Geba**. These films at the core of Wakamatsu's cinematic oeuvre comprise a brutally experimental/primal apocalypse which transcends the limitations of exploitation yet still impacts with a visceral force unequalled by any comparable sequence in Western cinema. At implosion point, Wakamatsu's films transgress into a zone of pure cinema where logocentric notions of narrative are immolated and infernal meta-texts combust in the right brain like neural napalm.

1969's **Shojo Geba Geba** ("Geba Geba Virgin"[1]) is a stupendous 70-minute tour-de-force set in a desolate rural landscape which, it soon becomes apparent, represents an infernal circle of sex and violence from which there is no escape and in which all the pawns who play out Wakamatsu's cinematic schema are sentenced to either death or a purgatorial eternity of lost souls.

The film opens in black and white with shots and freeze-frames of a night city set to a fractured percussive soundtrack, then cuts to two cars – one white, one black – speeding along the dirt roads of some bleak, deserted terrain. In the first car, three men hold a fourth, tied and blindfolded, captive. When they stop and pull the man out to urinate, the second car is shown to be full of jeering young women. Both cars then arrive at a barren, windswept spot marked by a huge wooden crucifix. A blindfolded woman is dragged from the second car and she and the blindfolded man are hurled into a gulley together. Despite his bonds, the man gropes the woman's crotch. The girls from the car, secretly watching, strip the couple semi-naked. The couple kiss, pondering their fate. We learn that the man, Hochi, works for a yakuza boss; he has made the mistake of having an affair with the boss's girlfriend, Hanako, and now they are both doomed to die. They are next stripped completely naked, as the girls continue their voyeuristic vigil.

Finally the couple are pulled apart; Hanako, her blindfold removed, is lashed to the crucifix. Hochi is dragged up to look at her before being untied and shoved into a tent. Soon one of the girls enters the tent, strips naked and starts to make love to him, lasciviously pawing his body. Cut to the other girls jeering at Hanako on the cross. Cut back to the tent, where Hochi is now throttling the girl, strangling her to death. He slips beneath the back of the tent into the gulch and flees for his life. The thugs soon discover the girl's corpse and give chase to Hochi in their car, but he reaches terrain where they cannot follow. They give up, cursing him.

Hochi flees into the distance, gasping and screaming in horror. We follow his flight for several miles, across barren tracts to the horizon. Here he collapses in exhaustion, and drifts into sleep haunted by Hanako calling his name. In a green-tinted sequence, soundless but for a musical track, he dreams of her being gang-raped by the thugs, next to the nude corpse of the strangled girl. She escapes, runs into the fields as the sequence erupts into full colour. Reunited, they make love, but as her hand caresses Hochi's back she suddenly feels an animal's tail growing from the base of his spine. Hochi wakes up abruptly.

For hours he wanders the wasteland, dressed only in the strangled girl's slip, tormented. Then, as

daylight fades and the full fist of night balls into black, he encounters another group of people encamped on a hilltop. These men are dressed in fine suits and surrounded by naked concubines. Hochi is welcomed, fed, fondled by the girls. He is shown a rifle, mounted on a fixed tripod, with telescopic sights. Through the sights he sees a girl's breast and nipple, no more. They urge him to pull the trigger. He complies, firing a shot into the dark, and is rewarded by sex with both the whores.

In the morning the group are seen dressing, shaving, the girls exercising naked in the early sun. After they all pose for group photos by automatic camera, Hochi wanders off. Cut to him returning to the original site, greeted with unbridled hostility by the vicious, vengeful thugs. He ignores them, seeing only (in colour) Hanako, still slumped on the cross, with a bullet wound in her right breast. Blood is pouring the length of her body. She seems to be still alive. Hochi catches her blood in his cupped hands. Intercut with the thugs in black and white shots. Back to colour as Hochi realises it was he who shot her; it was her breast in the rifle sights. He drinks her blood as if in expiation. From this moment on Hochi seems to possess a messianic aura. His presence triggers mass psychosis, fear. We see him next in the tent, making necrophiliac advances to the strangled girl. The thugs strip their girlfriends naked, one by one, and shove them into the tent where Hochi brutally rapes them in turn as the dead girl "watches". Two of the girls flee and are pursued by two of the thugs. The third man sees Hanako stir on the cross and flees in atavistic terror.

Rifle shots. The men in suits pick off the fleeing girls and also open fire on the two remaining thugs, who head back to the crucifixion site. Cut to Hochi, who is now encased from head to toe in a sack, writhing like a chrysalis behind the cross. Nude female corpses litter the ground around him. The thugs set upon him with baseball bats, beating him to an apparent pulp as the sack darkens with blood. Then, in homicidal frenzy, they set upon each other. One destroys the other's skull and then himself collapses dead. There are now corpses everywhere.

Hanako stirs, calls for Hochi. Miraculously still alive, he responds from the sack. A valedictory dialogue ensues, until Hanako finally expires from her wound. A bizarre ballad strikes up on the soundtrack.

Eventually the men in suits arrive, whores in tow. Gloating over the carnage of this nightmare Golgotha, they pose for more self-portraits in front of the crucified Hanako. Hochi silently emerges from the sack, baseball bat in hand. He has realised that the men are yakuza, and that the one who urged him to pull the trigger was in fact his boss – whose face he had never been allowed to see. In a quick series of freeze-frames showing the yakuza group posing in front of the cross, we see Hochi emerging behind them, ever nearer, his face a mask of twisted hate, until the screen erupts with the film's final, cathartic violence. Hochi brutally slays the entire group, girls included, finally dragging the boss to the foot of the crucifix where he caves in his skull like an eggshell.

A storm breaks. The field is now littered with bloody corpses. Return to colour for the final sequence. As the strange ballad once again strikes up, we see the cross in flames, as if blasted by lightning. Sporadic fires pock the terrain. Hochi bears his lover's body away through this blazing, apocalyptic landscape to vanishing-point.

In **Shojo Geba Geba** Wakamatsu employs customary devices – freeze-frames, white light, idiosyncratic soundtracking, jump cuts, colour segments to denote temporal, emotional or perspective shifts, and provocative widescreen compositions – to produce a cinema whose marriage of terse economic and virulent aesthetic has seldom been rivalled. Thematically, he clearly prefigures Pasolini's **Salo**, both in his claustrophobic depictions of ineluctable, internecine sexual violence and in his implicit political assertion that beyond the law lies only an even deadlier noose of fascistic repression. In **Geba**, his psychosis finally achieves a truly religious intensity; Wakamatsu has produced the ultimate fusion of his terrifying, revolutionary obsessions.

1. "Geba" has no literal translation. It derives from the German "gewalt", meaning strength or power, and is a political term used by leftist Japanese students to describe their movement (e.g. geba-bo ["staffs of power"], the long sticks used in violent encounters with police). A phonetic spelling of "gay bar" has also been posited as the word's meaning in **Shojo Geba Geba**'s title; since the title was reportedly suggested to Wakamatsu by Nagisa Oshima, a political connotation seems much more likely. For Wakamatsu's 1998 retrospective in Tokyo, the film was shown under the English title **Violent Virgin**.

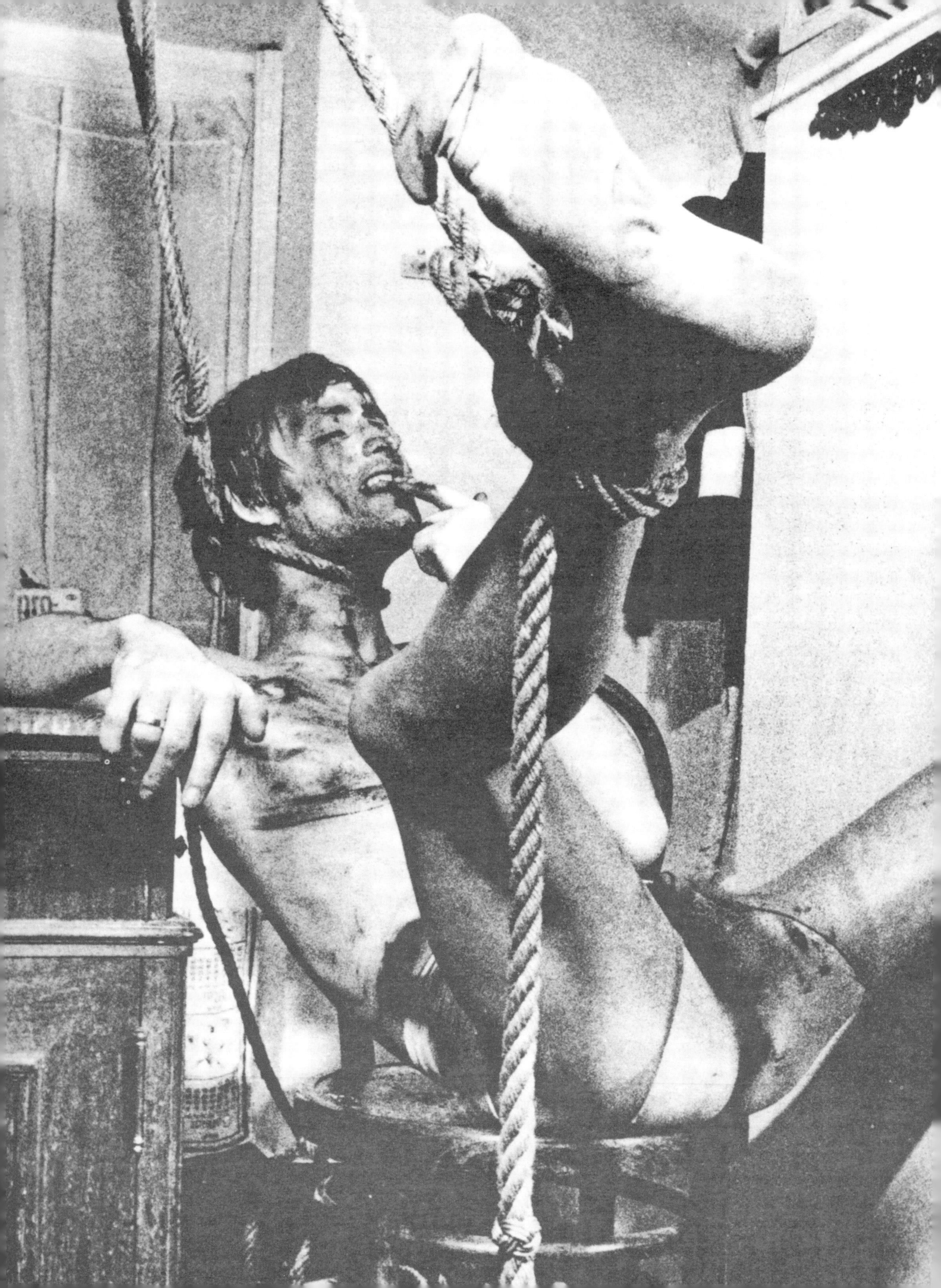

the films of the vienna action group

The Vienna Action Group generated a body of films which are unique – in their contrary forms, strategies and preoccupations – as the essential counterpart to a twentieth-century performance art movement. The Action Group were not the first such movement to recognise the potential of cinema – from the Dada and Italian Futurist movements of the first decades of the century onwards, the realization of performance through its transmission into film images had been a primary preoccupation; but that preoccupation often initially mediated itself through film manifestoes (or, in the case of the Futurists, through film-experiments which are now lost), rather than via a tangible body of performance-impelled films. In the mid-1950s, a decade before the Vienna Action Group's films, the Japanese Gutai movement in Osaka had often documented their performance actions (such as those of Kazuo Shiraga and Saburo Murakami, with their acts of corporeal struggle and annihilation against the media of paper-screens and mud) with super-8 films; but those films served essentially to carry the linear documentation of actions, rather than existing as works which fired autonomously from the performances that they confronted. Throughout the period until the open availability of video-cameras in the 1970s, the medium of photography remained dominant in documenting performance art worldwide; the traces of the Action Group's work vitally pivot between photography and film, with the work of the highly-professional commercial photographer Ludwig Hoffenreich (used by the Action Group artists precisely for its cold, objective beauty) forming the pre-eminent photographic representation of their actions, both in black-and-white and colour images. By contrast, the filmmakers allied to the Action Group formed active participants and collaborators in their work, often immersed as intensively in corporeal and visual experimentation and provocation as the artists themselves, and incurring some of the same reactions of social retribution as a result.

Although two filmmakers in particular – Kurt Kren and Ernst Schmidt Jr – became entangled in the Action Group's work in the mid-1960s to the extent that (in Kren's case) the still-discernible division between artist and filmmaker disintegrated to some degree, the Action Group also intermittently filmed their own actions or those of one another, seeking to eliminate the intervening element of representation which presented an impediment to their actions: the Action Group's films often emerge as mutating counterparts to their actions, rather than as the secondary documentation of those actions. Particularly in the final collaborations between Muehl and Kren, from the end of the 1960s and beginning of the 1970s (at the time when Muehl had largely abandoned his public actions and was consolidating his experiments in communal life), a more open equivalence is reached between artist and filmmaker: in those films of gleeful acts of sexual and excremental furore, such as **Sodoma** (1969) and **Shit-Bastard** (1970), both Muehl and Kren appear as prominent figures within the film image (animatedly sodomizing the other participants, or being soaked in and made to drink liquid excrement), and the artist/filmmaker division evanesces.

During the period when the films of the Action Group were made, those films were occasionally projected together as spectacles in their own right, within the same spaces in Vienna – cellars, insalubrious clubs and art-galleries – which also formed the venues for the Action Group's performances; they were, however, not

 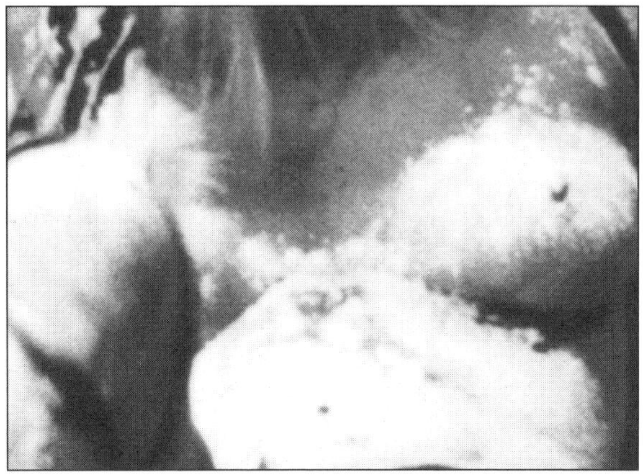

screened during that period at the Austrian Film Museum in Vienna, despite the prominent engagement of its young director, Peter Kubelka, in experimental and structuralist film. The films of the Action Group – as intensive ocular and sensorial assaults on their spectators – were certainly never conceived to be projected in commercial cinema spaces, and programmes of experimental film staged within European museums of modern art were then extremely limited; the films acquired an itinerance and haphazardness in their projection, screened at that time before wild or drunken audiences at events which also incorporated small-scale actions staged to complement the film-screenings. Hermann Nitsch also occasionally projected films of his previous actions during the actual performance of new actions, imparting to film the quality of a seminal reference or launching-point in generating his obsessions from one action to the next. In the following decades, the films were shown intermittently at experimental film collectives such as Anthology Film Archives in New York and the Film-makers' Co-operative in London, in programmes that also encompassed far less spectacular film works concerned insularly with the nature of film itself. After his departure from Vienna in the 1970s, Kren would become the embodiment of the films' uprooted itinerance, endlessly travelling between American university campuses to screen his films of the Action Group to audiences of art students. It was only with the elevation of experimental film as a prominent art form in its own right, and the institution of large-scale film programmes within contemporary art venues, in the late 1980s and early 1990s, that the Action Group's films began to regain a strong public visibility.

In the films of the Action Group, the impact carried by the sensory power of blood in performance is also carried by film itself: film materializes into an overwhelming and multiple substance, as capable of exacting resonances and responses on profoundly contrary and insurgent levels as is the blood unleashed in the act of performance: corporeal, mystical, ecstatic, societal and aesthetic levels. Blood forms a pivotal rip in the temporal duration of a performance: the deluge it inflicts upon the action's participants engenders an excessive calamity (often accompanied by the raw impetus of a sexual act in Muehl's performances, or by the sudden revelation of the healing of a crisis in Nitsch's performances); film too forms a point of visual overload from which all acts and elements of existence must be entirely reconfigured by the overhauled spectator. Blood and film also possess their gratuitous powers: in the flow of blood over the body in performance, that body becomes subject to a multiplicity of chance movements – each recuperable only in the film image – that all carry their own arbitrary, chaotic charge. And on a primary level, blood forms a powerfully glaring colour, in its collision both with the human body and with the film image that collects it. In the mixing of blood (human and animal blood is infinitely

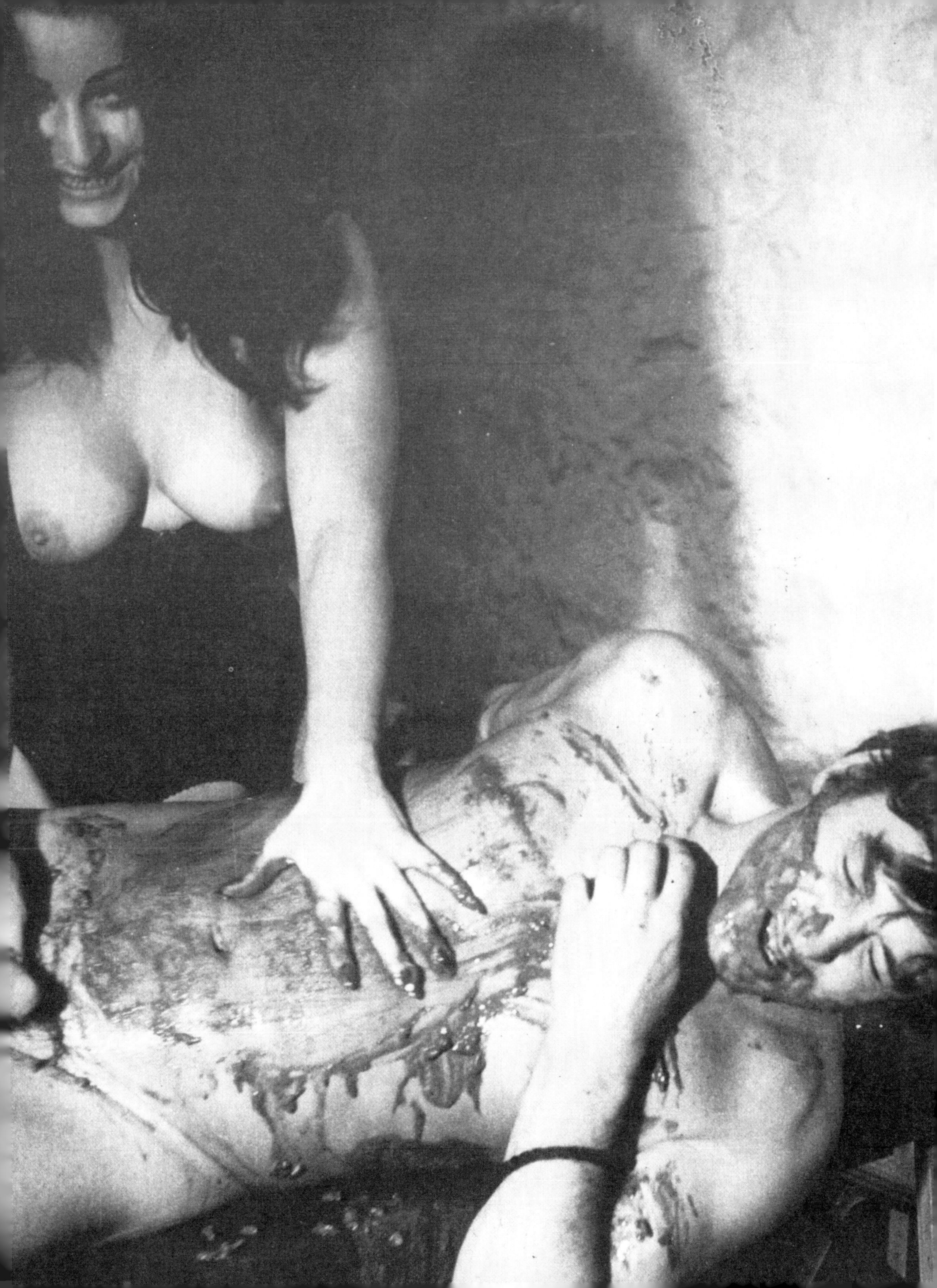

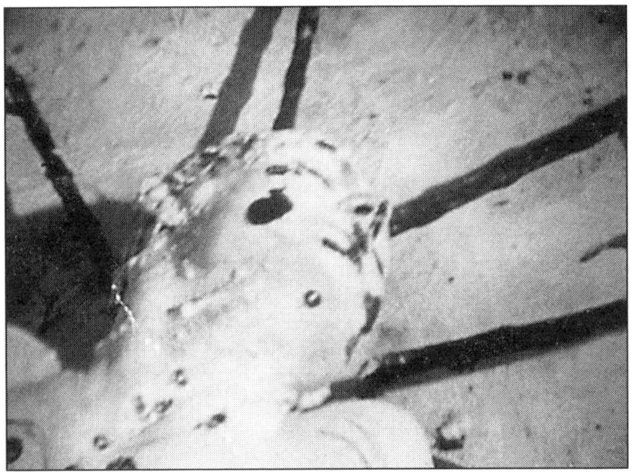

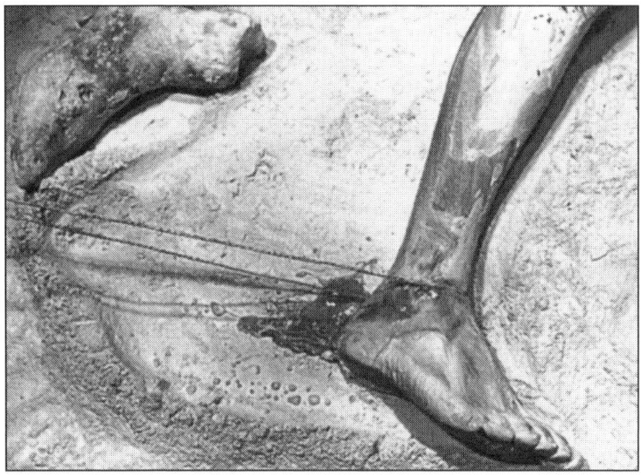

mixed in the Action Group's performances, with semen, urine, excrement, and other liquids and substances), an irreparable disruption of vision is generated both for the performance's spectator and for the film's spectator; even the potential healing of such a disruption, in the actions of Nitsch, forms a violent infiltration and erasure of the body, the dynamic scope of which can be rendered only by film. In the work of the Action Group, film constitutes the amalgam of corporeal debris and fragments accumulated within the image; however brief in duration that accretion of textures and layers may be (a fraction of a second in Kren's films), it hooks into its spectator's perception. The spectator's eye then itself forms a screen, of horror, delight or fascination, for the impact of the action on film; and crucially, in the urgency of its rapport with film, that eye forms a lens of death with the aperture only momentarily open.

In the 1960s, the potential of film to carry such intricate resonances as those of bloodshed in performance was linked in the perception of filmmakers – including the Action Group's principal collaborators, Kren and Schmidt Jr – to the celluloid film-stock itself, which became imprinted with the image of the performance, and also with damage inflicted by the scratchings, amendments or attacks of the filmmaker's own hand. As in the experimental film culture of the same era in the United States, in the work of such diverse filmmakers as Kenneth Anger, Hollis Frampton and George Landow, the celluloid film-stock used for the Action Group's films itself possessed its own magical aura as the receptive but capricious medium for the filmmaker's obsessions. In the period before the video and digital image, the variability attached to celluloid film-stock constituted a pre-eminent means to explore the chance form of performance actions: the film image remained vitally unknown and subject to infinite deviation until it had been developed and projected. Even then, that vulnerable celluloid would go on to receive and accumulate the scars of each future public projection, just as the bodies of the Action Group's participants held the physical or mental woundings of their intensive acts. In Japan during the same period of the mid-1960s, the experimental filmmaker Takahiko Iimura evolved a particular strategy in his films of performance actions, such as those he made of the work of the choreographer Tatsumi Hijikata, undertaking what he termed 'cine-dances', in which he moved freely around the performance with his film camera, catching partial fragments which then transmitted a force of corporeal elation and visual compulsion to the resulting films (whose developed celluloid he then also subjected to manual assaults). The films of the Action Group's performances hold a parallel experimentation upon the substance and potential of celluloid itself, to render the chance gestures, ecstasy and raw fury of the actions.

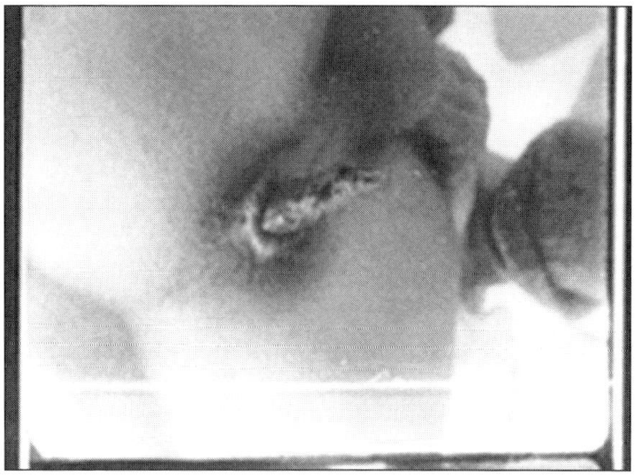

Although the Action Group artists maintained a high level of public visibility in Vienna in the second half of the 1960s, with the exception of Schwarzkogler, their principal filmic collaborators – Kren and Schmidt Jr – remained far less prominent (as was the case too with their principal photographic collaborator, Ludwig Hoffenreich). Those filmmakers' involvement with the Action Group imparted a degree of notoriety to their work – Kren in particular shared some of the Action Group's persecution by the Vienna police – but gave them few financial or aesthetic rewards. While Brus and Nitsch, in particular, had become viewed as successful art-market celebrities by the end of the 1980s, with large-scale retrospectives of their work in prospect, both Kren and Schmidt Jr remained largely peripheral, isolated presences. Despite that obscurity, they formed essential figures in the original creation of the Action Group's work, and also in the survival and enduring virulence of that work.

the execution of ion victor antonescu

A particularly detailed, almost sadistic film document of the execution by firing squad on June 1, 1946 of ousted Romanian dictator Ion Antonescu, along with three of his chief collaborators. Antonescu, a close ally of Hitler and a professed anti-Semite believed responsible for the extermination of over 400,000 Jews and gypsies, first seized power in 1940 but was toppled in 1944. After a spell in a Russian prison he was handed back to Romania for trial, and sentenced to death for war crimes by a people's tribunal, along with three others (Constantin Z. Vasiliu, Gheorghe Alexiano and Mihai Antonescu). The military film of the execution shows the four men being led to a forest clearing where they are made to stand up against stakes. Antonescu defiantly raises his hat before all four are shot down in a hail of bullets. They are not all dead however, and an officer steps forward and shoots them in the head with a pistol, one by one. One man even requires a further headshot by rifle, before the doctor is satisfied. The camera then closes in on the bloody corpses and faces of the dead, lingering over staring eyes, gore-smeared mouths, and contorted limbs.

"fuses": a film by carolee schneemann

Carolee Schneemann, the radical performance artist whose 60s events included *Meat Joy* – a semi-naked orgy with blood, plastic, dead chickens and fish – here produces a pornographic, self-shot document of her and her lover fucking, turning it into art by treating the celluloid with acid, colouring, scratching and even cooking, before subjecting it to a cut-up process that renders everything down to a random, amorphous pulse. Shot and created between 1964 and 1967, and running for around 20 minutes, **Fuses** explores the fractured consciousness of sexual ecstasy in a construct which often recalls the film experiments of Kurt Kren and the Vienna Actionists, shot during the same period, both approaching a moment of annihilation through physical transcendence in grievously reconfigured time.

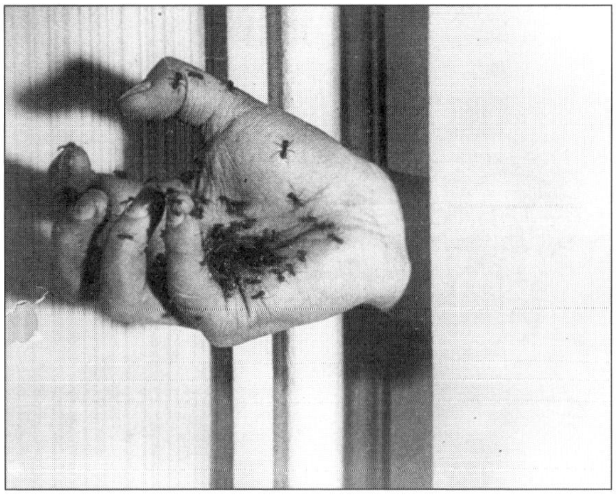 

"un chien andalou"

Un Chien Andalou, though primarily a subjective drama fashioned into a poem, is none the less, in my opinion, a film of social consciousness.

Un Chien Andalou is a masterwork from every aspect: its certainty of direction, its brilliance of lighting, its perfect amalgam of visual and ideological associations, its sustained dream-like logic, its admirable confrontation between the subconscious and the rational.

Considered in terms of social consciousness, **Un Chien Andalou** is both precise and courageous.

Incidentally I would like to make the point that it belongs to an extremely rare class of film.

I have met M. Luis Buñuel only once and then only for ten minutes, and our meeting in no way touched upon **Un Chien Andalou**. This enables me to discuss it with that much greater liberty. Obviously my comments are entirely personal. Possibly I will get near the truth, without doubt I will commit some *faux pas*.

In order to understand the significance of the film's title it is essential to remember that M. Buñuel is Spanish.

An Andalusian dog howls – who then is dead?

Our cowardice, which leads us to accept so many of the horrors that we, as a species, commit, is dearly put to the test when we flinch from the screen image of a woman's eye sliced in half by a razor. Is it more dreadful than the spectacle of a cloud veiling a full moon?

Such is the prologue: it leaves us with no alternative but to admit that we will be committed, that in this film we will have to view with something more than the everyday eye.

Throughout the film we are held in the same grip.

From the first sequence we discern, beneath the image of an overgrown child riding up the street without touching the handlebars, hands on his thighs, covered with white frills like so many wings, we discern, I repeat, our truth which turns to cowardice in contact with the world which we accept, (one gets the world one deserves), this world of inflated prejudices, of betrayals of one's inner self, of pathetically romanticised regrets.

M. Buñuel is a fine marksman who disdains the stab in the back.

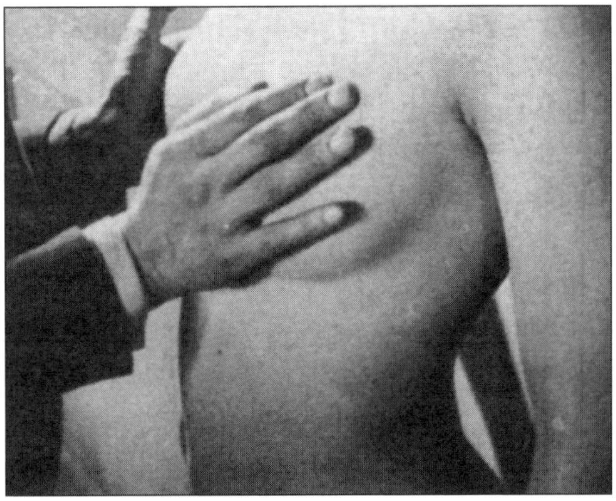

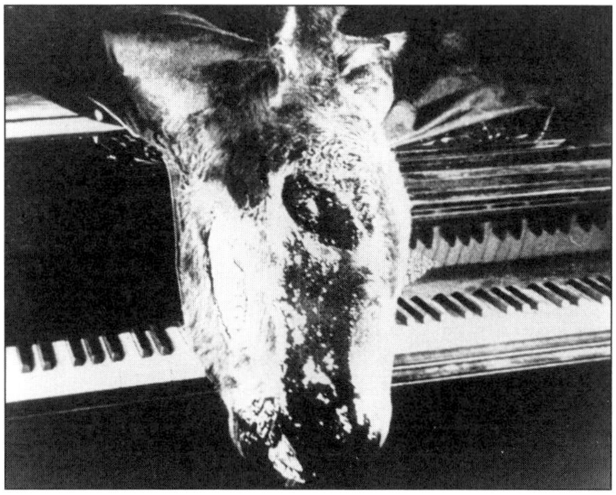

A kick in the pants to macabre ceremonies, to those last rites for a being no longer there, who has become no more than a dust filled hollow down the centre of the bed.

A kick in the pants to those who have sullied love by resorting to rape.

A kick in the pants to sadism, of which buffoonery is its most disguised form.

And let us pluck a little at the reins of morality with which we harness ourselves.

Let's see a bit of what is at the end.

A cork, here is a weighty argument.

A melon – the disinherited middle classes.

Two priests – alas for Christ!

Two grand pianos, stuffed with corpses and excrement – our pathetic sentimentality!

Finally, the donkey in close up. We were expecting it.

M. Buñuel is terrible.

Shame on those who kill in youth what they themselves would have become, who seek in the forests and along the beaches, where the sea casts up our memories and regrets.the dried up projection of their first blossoming. *Cave canem...*

Beware of the dog – it bites.

All this written in an attempt to avoid too arid an analysis, image by image, in any case impossible in a good film whose savage poetry exacts respect – and with the sole aim of creating the desire to see or see again **Un Chien Andalou**. To cultivate a socially aware cinema is to ensure a cinema which deals with subjects which provoke interest, of subjects which cut ice ...

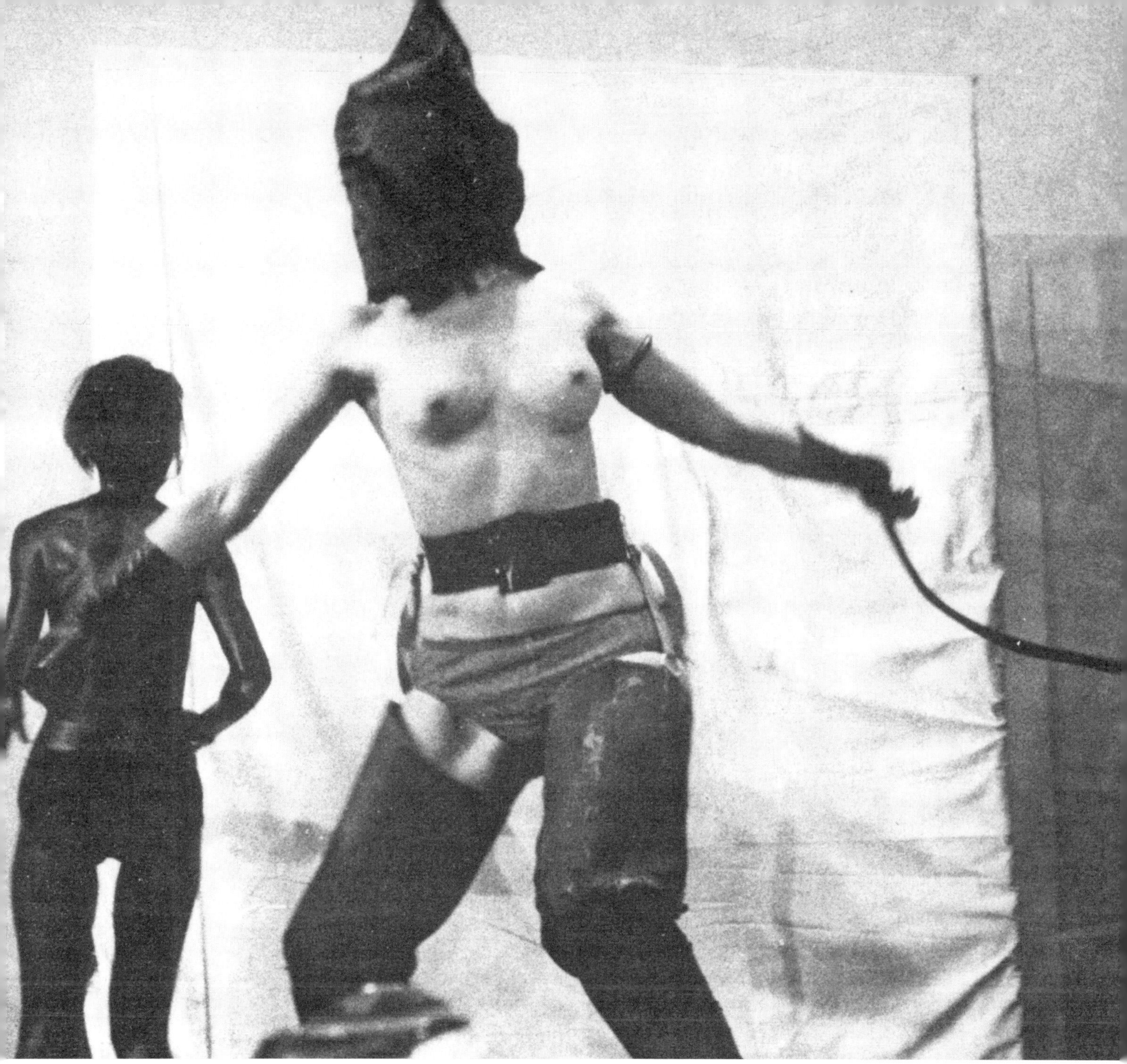

documents of panic: "he viva dada"

When the Chilean theatre director Alejandro Jodorowsky came to 1960s Paris in search of the Surrealists, he found them in a state of nullification. Disgusted and disillusioned, he joined forces with writer Fernando Arrabal and artist Roland Topor to found the Panic Movement, a super-Dadaist, confrontational (though essentially parodic) performance manifesto, and inaugurated a series of bizarre Panic Happenings throughout the city. These were staged orgies of sadism and blasphemy, featuring dead animals, topless dancers and whip bitches and set to freeform rock, which culminated in the outrageous, 4-hour "Sacramental Melodrama" at the Festival Of Free Expression in 1965. **He Viva Dada**, filmed by Jean-Michel Humeau, was a startling, black-and-white visual document of a Panic Happening at the Parisian American Centre that same year.

mishima: death-fragments

In a television interview recorded in 1969, the year before his death by self-disembowelment and decapitation by one of his acolytes, Yukio Mishima spoke of how 'an extreme form of eroticism' had always driven his life, unleashed by his experiences of Tokyo under warfare and the sensation of imminently-expected death he experienced there, and carrying him far beyond the stratified parameters of Japanese literary and cultural life, as though that life had been choreographed towards death, by his close friend of the 1960s, the instigator of Ankoku Butoh dance, Tatsumi Hijikata – as a set of compulsive gestures, simultaneously pathological and exquisite, and propelled, too, outside the anticipated boundaries of the corporeal and the rigorously annotated sensory categories of Japan, always a hairsbreadth away from both orgasm and erasure.

Three years before his death, Mishima wrote *The Way Of The Samurai* from his lifelong engagement with the *Hagakure*, an eighteenth-century manual on samurai life, compiled in the form of fragments imparted by a now-retired samurai (who had expected to be allowed to commit ritual suicide on the death of his master, but through an anomaly, was prevented from doing so, and chose instead to distance himself from life) and transcribed by a young auditor. The *Hagakure* is a set of austere interdictions about the necessity of the samurai's readiness for death at every moment, but it also contains elements of gratuitous contradictions, black holes of nihilism, as though the profound rigour of samurai life, and its ultimate futility (as in the comparison the manual draws with puppetry-gestures) together form part of the same movement of implosion.

In exploring the *Hagakure*, Mishima refines the material that is vital for his own death: the act of death that engulfs every gestural act, every creative act, every sexual act, reversing in time to simultaneously validate and erase all of those prior acts. Mishima is always irresistibly compelled, almost unable to restrain himself for another instant, from his act of death; as in the theoretical texts and novels of Georges Bataille, if every act of outrage, excess and death-obsession cannot be concentrated into an identical moment of life, now, then everything must be done to ensure that it will happen in the next moment of life. What French philosophers such as Jacques Derrida and Julia Kristeva learned from their reading of Mishima is that, if death cannot be carried through immediately (the state of perpetual suspension which is that of the samurai's life), then it must, at least, be made the sole focus of representation: representation with its own cancellation engrained within the obsession to expose, to transmit, to project.

The year before writing *The Way Of The Samurai*, Mishima had co-directed a film which represents and anticipates his ritual suicide, acted by himself, though without the participation of his private army of erotically-uniformed young men, the Shield Society, who accompanied him in 1970 on his death-mission to the Ichigaya barracks in Tokyo. The pre-eminent writer on contemporary Japan, and close friend of Mishima, Donald Richie, attended the shooting of Mishima's film, and remembered: 'In time, he asked me to come to the Daiei film studio… The movie, **The Rite Of Love And Death (Yukoku)**, based on the short story 'Patriotism', was already half-completed and this was the second day of filming. A container of pig intestines stood ready and after rehearsal, these were packaged inside Mishima's trousers. When the knife seemed to enter the author's abdomen it actually cut into the plastic sack containing the guts… This transformation was strong.'

Mishima's film is pitched so tightly at the interstice between orchestrated sexual bliss and blood-drenched corporeal chaos, with its loving shots of his own thighs, muscled chest, barely-covered penis, immediately before the act of self-laceration, that it exceeds and annuls all linear narration, and projects itself in the form of a sensorially-attuned sequence of fragments – exactly the same form he sets to work in *The Way Of The Samurai* for his exploration of the *Hagakure*. All language, all image, must be dismantled, disassembled, into the form of

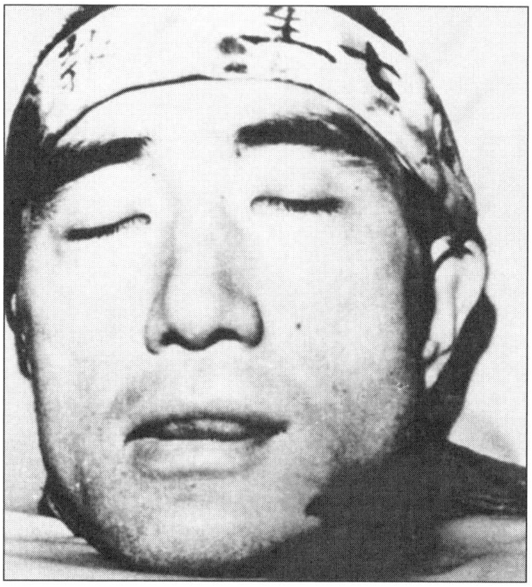

the fragment, so that it detaches itself from its tainting by its habitual social misuse, in order to become the medium of pure obsession, perpetual orgasm, with the instant of the onrush of death sustained into infinity.

In *The Way Of The Samurai*, Mishima contrasts the eighteenth-century samurai era with that of contemporary Japan (that of 1967, a year poised between the two ratifications of the US-Japan Security Treaty, which had rendered Japan an obsequious client-state of the USA, and shortly before the great end-of-the-decade era of violent street-riots which Mishima lived to witness, but rejected as just one more void consumer-experience), tellingly castigating a city in which consumerism-induced frenzies have overridden the grandeur and stature he wants to accord to the corporeal, in its moment before death: 'Throughout Tokyo, pygmy romances are rampant today.' In doing so, he creates a parallel with the temporal system of the Hagakure, in which the retired samurai laments an era, thirty years before, in which samurai warriors had been authentic, and had not been consumed only by thoughts of wealth and 'effeminacy'. A gap of time must always be generated, in Mishima's obsessions, in order for the contemporary moment to be conjured into such vilification, that the only recourse is death.

Mishima experiences those boundaries of time as spatial boundaries, too. In his conversations with Donald Richie, he projected himself into the excessive time and space of imperial Rome, but also into a contemporary space of Tokyo denied to him: that of the sexual and alcohol-driven sensory furore of the down-at-heel San'ya district. Donald Richie recalls: 'Mishima sometimes said he felt so cut off from the things he really liked. He said that some time in Rome under Tiberius would have been interesting. Or maybe Diacletian – he was thinking of Sebastian. He toyed with the idea of reincarnation – not seriously, but as a kind of joke, wondered if he hadn't been a Persian slave boy in an earlier life, or an indulgent emperor. As for San'ya (a district something like the Bowery of Tokyo, home of the proletariat worker), here the barrier was spatial, not temporal. He could not go there because of who he had become. He would have been recognized.'

To reconcile his unique time and space, and to project it to the world as an act beyond representation, Mishima's final act of death forms the embodiment of that 'extreme form of eroticism' which led, as he said in the same television interview of 1969, to 'a proud form of death': 'Harakiri makes you win.' In the police photographs of the aftermath of Mishima's death, in which his severed head had been placed upright, on a cloth, alongside that of one of his Shield Society acolytes, and photographed in close-up, his face emanates an oblivion that has passed through every corporeal, sensory and sexual aperture, in order to mediate his obsession, stopped-dead in that instant of raw bliss, for the eye of his reader and spectator.

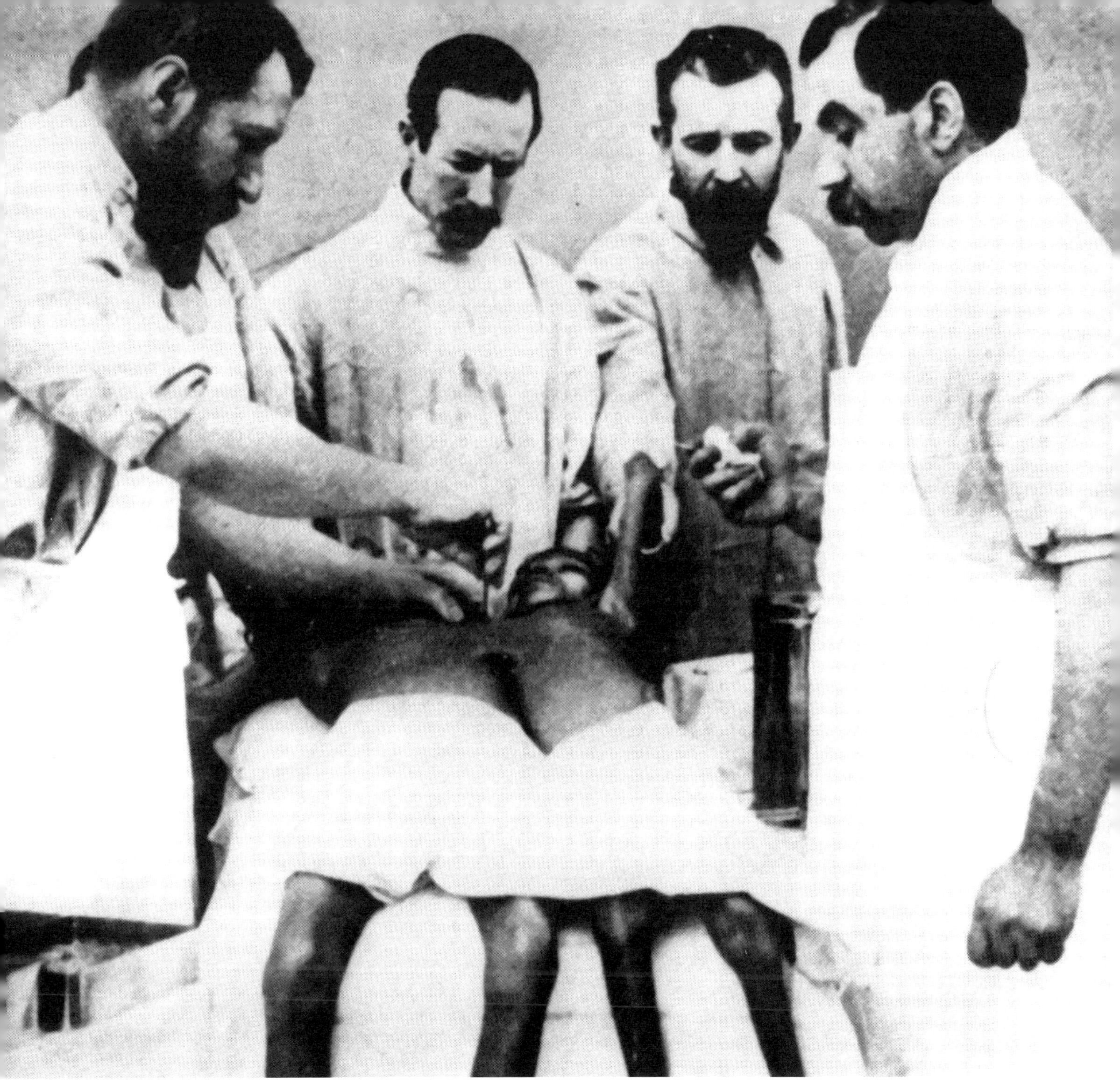

"the separation of radica and doodica"

The pioneer of medical gore cinema, Eugène-Louis Doyen was the first surgeon to film his operations, including such graphic procedures as craniectomies and hysterectomies; his most celebrated film, shot in Paris in 1902, was of the separation of famed Indian xiphopages (Siamese twins) Radica and Doodica. The operation was initially successful, although both twins were dead within a year. Doyen later found himself at the centre of controversy when it was discovered that some of his films were being secretly distributed by Ambroise-François Parnaland, his cameraman/producer, with copies being projected at fairground freakshows.

albert speer: "hitler's buildings"

Hitler's Buildings (**Die Bauten Adolf Hitlers**) is a 17-minute, 1938 propaganda film by the visionary Nazi architect Albert Speer, concerning the "racial superiority" and purity of Hitler's construction program from 1934 onwards. Condemning "modern" building designs as decadent, Speer presents monumental stone edifices with intrinsic "ruin value", designed to last for one thousand years; as he wrote earlier in a 1936 article entitled *Die Bauten des Führers*: "The buildings of our Führer will speak of the greatness of our age to future millennia". Speer's works for Hitler included the Reich Chancellery and the *Zeppelinhaupttribüne* in Nuremberg, with its spectacular "Hall of Pillars". Many of Hitler's and Speer's most audacious projects remained unrealised; these include *Welthauptstadt Germania*, a radical rebuilding of Berlin as the capital city of the world, and Hitler's own death monument in Linz, his birthplace, a vertiginous tower atop which would rest the twin sarcophagi of the Führer and his consort, Eva Braun, literally overlooking the entire world for eternity. Speer was later the subject of Joachim Fest's TV documentary **Der Architekt** (1969), and Brian Nolan's **The Last Nazi** (1976), in which interviews are intercut with wartime footage and home movies as Speer reflects on his life with, and after Hitler.

the rape of architecture by drama

Carl Dreyer has argued that the cinema's closest relative is architecture.

It may seem paradoxical to compare the most mimetic (photographic) of the arts with the construction of a new reality, and a dramatic art with a 'Utopian' one. Equally unexpected is the *rapprochement* of the most fluid of all visual media with the most solid and static.

Yet the paradoxes hold. For, by its nature, the cinema is a *beau monstre*. Like the theatre, it centres on actors. *But* its tempo-spatial flexibility approaches the novel's. *But* it is predominantly visual – flat, like painting. *But* its visuals exist in *movement* and *time*, so that its plasticity has musical components. *But* its photographic quality precludes music abstraction, suggesting a very literal realism. *But* seeing a film is notoriously a dream-like experience.

This blend of realism and oneirism provides the clue to Dreyer's meaning. The cinema's mimetic fullness (photography, movement, sound) permits the creation of a *self-sufficient* world. Like the architect, the film director weaves diverse media into a 'new' reality.

The traditional division between the 'dramatic' and the other arts is only part of the story. Dramatic ugliness and tensions, even the tragic end, occur within aesthetic 'distance' and form part of an ultimately agreeable existence. The character dies, but author and actors enjoy our enthusiastic applause. Through vicarious experience, katharsis and enhanced understanding, drama, like architecture, improves the world.

And architecture, in its way, implies drama. There is the possibility of displeasure. An effective building, like a circus acrobat, might be graceless, but flies through the air with the greatest of ease. Its 'suspense' is non-representational, but exists as intensely as that of music. As Keats and Freud agreed, there is no beauty without melancholy, no thrill without anxiety, no elegance without the remembrance of pain. Creativity treads a tightrope between complacent 'good taste' (too little 'danger') and bad taste (an emotional 'unhappy end').

Architecture's immobility makes it the natural complement of the movie-camera. The basic architectural experiences – standing in a space, looking around, and walking along a corridor – find their equivalents in the screen frame, in the panning shot (the camera turns its head), and the tracking shot (the camera walks forward or backwards). Though the screen is flat, the camera's reticulation of movements in space confer on the succession of images (the sequence) a quality of space-in-depth, controlled and orchestrated.

Architecture has been described as 'frozen music'. When the camera moves, the roofline flows past us like a river. The camera tilts rapidly up, and banister and staircase cascade down. The cinema is 'unfrozen architecture'.

In the opening shots of Thorold Dickinson's **Overture** the swooping camera counterpoints the inner lines of the U.N. building at Lake Success with the opening theme of Beethoven's *Egmont Overture*. Space becomes time, balconies and musical phrases leap out together. The cinema *is* an architecture (and is the best medium for recording architecture).[1]

1. But film hurls form into a melting-pot of its own. It abducts, reforms, deforms, all it shows. Jean Cocteau's **Le Sang d'Un Poète** opens with a factory chimney beginning to fall. Seventy minutes later it concludes with the chimney hitting the ground. This 'time-split' establishes the oneirism of the intervening story (for back in the 30's dreams were thought to be all but instantaneous). But it harnesses also the thrill and awed chill we feel watching demolitions. We hold our breath, because as the chimney falls, we fall. That crumbling chimney is the spectator's own body 'dissolving', and through kinaesthetic empathy it triggers emotions of failure and death.

the lost, aborted and fragmented films of kenneth anger

Kenneth Anger's film-making career has been marked by a series of films which were lost, stolen, destroyed, or abandoned due to lack of funds or other (often mysterious) circumstances. This pattern commenced soon after the completion of **Fireworks** (1947) when Anger failed to raise sufficient money to realise his next project, **Puce Women**, which was to be a feature-length film about fading Hollywood stars in their crumbling mansions. From trial footage shot in 1948, Anger was able to assemble and score a single fragment only, which he titled **Puce Moment**.

"**Puce Women** was my love affair with mythological Hollywood. A straight, heterosexual love affair, no bullshit, with all the great goddesses of the silent screen. They were to be filmed in their actual house; I was, in effect, filming ghosts." –Anger, quoted in Tony Rayns, "Dedication To Create Make Believe".

PUCE MOMENT (1949)
6 min. 35mm. Color. Sound (Music by Jonathan Halper). Filmed in Hollywood.
Credits: Conceived, Directed, Photographed and Edited by Kenneth Anger. Cast: Yvonne Marquis (Star).

THE LOVE THAT WHIRLS (1949)
Color (Kodachrome).
No credits available. Film destroyed by Eastman-Kodak developing plant, who objected to nudity in simulated Mexican fertility rites. "*The Love That Whirls* was inspired by Frazer's *Golden Bough* and was about a human sacrifice – specifically an Aztec ritual in which a youth is chosen to be king... After one year, the day comes when the King is sacrificed..." –Anger, quoted in Rebekah Wood, "Notes On The Hidden Cinema Of Kenneth Anger"

LE JEUNE HOMME ET LA MORT (1951)
16mm. B&W. Silent. Filmed in Paris. From the ballet by Jean Cocteau.
Cast: Jean Babilee (Young Man); Nathalie Philipart (Death).
In 1951, Anger essayed the first of three abortive Paris projects which underscored his affinity with decadent French art and literature: Cocteau's *Le Jeune Homme Et La Mort*, Lautréamont's *Maldoror*, and *L'Histoire d'O* (*The Story Of O*) by Pauline Réage. Anger filmed this 16mm pilot in the hope of raising funds for a 35mm technicolor version but, despite Cocteau's full support, he failed.

LES CHANTS DE MALDOROR (1951–2)
From the novel by Isidore Ducasse, Le Comte de Lautréamont (1868).
No other credits available. Tests shots only, of the early "hymn to the ocean" segment (employing members of Marquis de Cuevas ballet), and a war between flies and pins. In addition to the customary lack of funds, Anger reported being intimidated by the Surrealists who were wary of an American filming their most revered text.

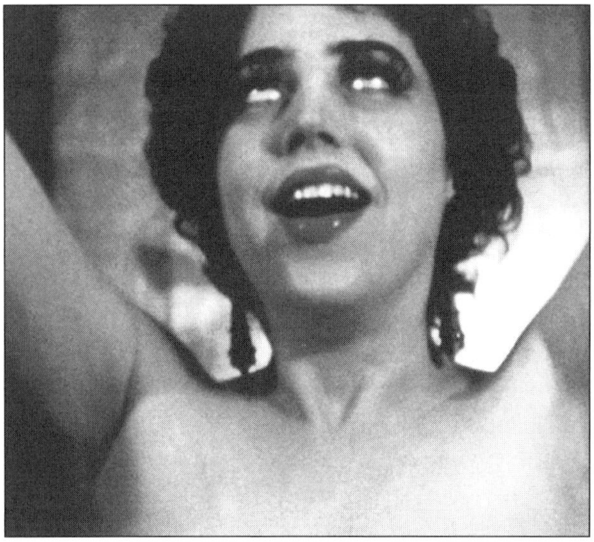

THELEMA ABBEY (1955)

10 min. B&W. Sound. Filmed in Thelema Abbey, Cefalu, Sicily.

A documentary by Kenneth Anger on the erotic frescoes in Aleister Crowley's ruined temple. The film was produced for British magazine *Picture Post*, who "lost" the documentary. Anger later described Crowley's paintings as "hyper-psychedelic murals: goblins and demons in fabulous colour, scarlet and pumpkin-red" (quoted in Rebekah Wood, "Notes On The Hidden Cinema Of Kenneth Anger")

L'HISTOIRE D'O (1961)

20 min. 16mm. B&W. Silent. Filmed in Paris. From the novel by Pauline Réage (1954).

Abandoned after Anger found out that money given to him by the boyfriend of the girl playing "O" was part of ransom paid out to kidnappers of Eric Peugeot, heir to the French automobile empire. It also transpired that the girl was the daughter of a priest, and when her parents heard about the film they immediately forbade her further participation. The story goes that the remaining footage is buried somewhere in France.

Anger returned to America in 1962 and, while living with underground film-makers Marie Menken and Willard Maas (Menken had directed the film dedication **Arabesque For Kenneth Anger** in 1961), made **Scorpio Rising**, his greatest – and most scandalous – success to date. As a result of the film's acclaim, Anger was awarded a $10,000 grant by the Ford Foundation – just before **Scorpio** was prosecuted for obscenity in Los Angeles. Part of this money went to the financing of Anger's next project, **Kustom Kar Kommandos**.

KUSTOM KAR KOMMANDOS (1964/5)

3 min. Color. Sound (Music by The Parris Sisters). Filmed in San Bernadino.

Cast: Sandy Trent (Car Customiser).

Fragment of an abandoned project. Failure to complete is attributed variously to lack of funds, Anger's nascent interest in psychedelia, and the death of the main actor in a drag race. Anger's original production notes read as follows:

"KUSTOM"

Film project by Kenneth Anger utilizing the Eastman rapid color emulsion Ektachrome ER, whose ASA rating of 125 opens up hitherto inaccessible realms of investigation in low-key color location work for the independent creative film-maker. Running time 30 minutes, track composed of pop music fragments combined with sync location-recorded sound effects and dialog.

KUSTOM is an oneiric vision of a contemporary American (and specifically Californian) teenage phenomenon, the world of the hot-rod and customized car. I emphasize the word "oneiric", as Kustom will not be a "documentary" covering the mechanical hopping-up and esthetic customizing of cars, but rather a dream-like probe into the psyche of the teenager for whom the "unique" aspect of the power potentialized customized car represents a poetic extension of personality, an accessible means of wish-fulfilmment. I will treat the custom cars created by the teenager and his adult mentors (such customizers as Ed Roth, Bill Cushenberry and George Barris, whose Kustom City in North Hollywood is a mecca of this world) as the objects of art – folk art if you prefer – that I consider them to be.

The aforementioned adult "mentors", most of whom are located in the periphery of Los Angeles and hence readily accessible for filming, will be shown at work in their body shops on various cars-in-the-process-of-becoming, in the role of "arch-priests" to the teenagers whose commission they are fulfilling. (The locales of body shops and garages will be presented uniquely in gleaming highlighted low-key, in a manner already essayed for the motorcycle garage locations of SCORPIO RISING); the idolized customizers (the only adults seen in the film) will be represented as shadowy, mysterious personages (priests or witch-doctors) while the objects of their creation, the cars, will bathe in a pool of multi-sourced (strictly non-realistic) light, an eye-magnet of nacreous color and gleaming curvilinear surfaces.

The treatment of the teenager in relation to his hot-rod or custom car (whether patiently and ingeniously fashioned by himself, as is usually the case, or commissioned according to his fantasy, for the economically favored) will bring out what I see as a definite "eroticization" of the automobile, in its dual aspect of narcissistic identification as virile power symbol and its more elusive role: seductive, attention-grabbing, gaudy or glittering mechanical mistress paraded for the benefit of his peers. (I am irresistably drawn to the comparison of these machines with an American cult-object of an earlier era, Mae West in her "Diamond Lil" impersonations of the Thirties).

The formal filmic construct of KUSTOM is planned as follows: (The division into titled "sections" is uniquely for working convenience; these divisions will be "erased" in the finished work.) The dominant pop record is indicated in capitals.

1 HAVE MONEY (The Young Conformers). An introduction insinuating the spectator into the teen-dream. A fast-shifting visual reverie utilizing the linking device of the lap-dissolve and the wipe to establish patterns of convention followed by the teenage (and sub-teen) group: similarity of hair-styling, style of dress, of language, attitude or manner, taste in dance patterns and pop music; the omniscience of certain popular heroes or ever-shifting masks on Archetypal Images.

2 DAWN (Crystalization). The concept of individual "style" dawns upon the Teenager. The carefully composed aerodynamics of a crested coiffure as it is formed. The love-lock. Raided sideburns. The embroidered, self-identifying jacket or painted T-shirt. The "far-out" color combinations in stove-pipe pants, shock-effect shirts and socks. The Grail: the vision of the Teenager as Owner of his own, screamingly individualistic, unique and personlized custom car. (These images of the Grail, "the goal", will be floated across the mirrored image of the Teenager as he arranges his coiffure or clothes.) Subliminal flashes as thumbs through hot-rod magazines or plays juke-box. Closeups of high-school desk tops showing open text books (Science or History) while adolescent hands doodle, first crudely, then with increasing refinement, silhouettes of hot-rod and custom "dream" cars.

3 THE NITTY-GRITTY (Realization). The Teenager attacks. Dream into action. Abrupt change in formal construct: sharp cuts, swift pans, darting dollies. The night-lit junk-yard, weird derelict cemetery: lifting a "goodie". The first jalopie: a rusty junked car pushed into the dark initiatory cave of the garbage. Series of car-framers in the process of being stripped: an almost savage dismantling (analogy to wild animals dismembering a carcass).

4 MY GUY (The Rite.) Under the occult guidance of the shadowy, mysterious adult customizers performing as Arch-Priest, the Teenager's Dream Car is born (allusion to obstetrics). The alchemical elements come into play: phosphorescent blue tongue of the welding flame, cherry glow of joins, spark shower of the buffer. Major operation: dropping the front, raising the back of the car, "channeling" and "chopping". The Priest-Surgeon (customizer) perfects the metal modulations from cardboard mock-ups; plunges in with blowtorch and mallet. The swooping sculpted forms (blackened and rough) materialize in closeups and their intent is perceived.

5 IN HIS KISS (The Adorning). Sudden darting color: the rainbow array as cans are opened, stirred dripping gaudy sticks held up for the Teenager's contemplation and approval. The iridescent "candy-flake" colors and shock-jewel tones in vogue. The Teenager chooses "his" color: tension, decision, joyful release. The cult-object – the shaping-up car body – in the swirl of colored spray-gun mists: rose and turquoise flourescent fogs as coat upon carefully-stroked, glittering coat, the car-body emerges as a radiant, gem-hued object of adoration. A reflected color-bath splashes over the absorbed faces of the watching teenagers: a whoop of triumph, a jungle-stomp of joy as the custom is "born".

6 WONDERFUL ONE (Possession). The Teenager takes possession of his own completed custom or hot-rod car: the painted finish is caressed, the line admired (as would be the line of a girl friend), the chromed shift fondled, firmly grasped. (For this kaleidoscopic montage involving scores of custom and hot-rod cars, it is hoped to include the outstanding examples of customizing currently touring America in the Ford Custom Car Caravan, which could well represent the ideal Dream Cars of America's custom-conscious teenagers. However, for their appearance in KUSTOM, it will be necessary to film them "in movement" against unified black or nocturnal backgrounds – an effect that can be accomplished by camera or optical artifice if it proves impractical to night-drive these valuable machines.)

7 THE FUGITIVE (Flight and Freedom). The Teenage hot-rodders "rev up" (The Syndrome of the Shift) and take off for a nocturnal drag race (irreal colored light-sources throughout). A lone hot-rodder races down a curving mountain road (Dead Man's Curve). The Custom Boys, "in slow motion", take command of the controls of their Dream Cars. (This concluding sequence of KUSTOM operates exclusively in the realm of "dream logic": it is intended to create a Science-Fictional atmosphere.) The hot-rodders experience the erotic power-ecstasy of the Shift (the Hurst shift will be employed) to the magnified accompaniment of motor and exhaust. The Custom Boys resemble Astronauts at their controls: their vari-hued craft seem to lift into space. (If possible, a prototype of an actual "air-car" by a noted West Coast designer will be utilized in this section.) The Dragsters streak down the search-light stabbed runway (ideally seen by helicopter) as in cross-cutting the Custom Boys are liberated into weightlessness with their strange craft, and plunge star-ward.

8 SHANGRI-LA (Apotheosis). The Dragsters streak towards an imposing podium (by montage inference) piled high with towering, animated trophies of glittering gold; the Custom Boys range above the golden mountain high and free. A nocturnal jostling cheering crowd of teenagers (lit by swinging stabbing searchlights) swing up on their shoulders The Winner – Mr.

Hot-Rod, his glowing triumpth-filled countenance streaming sweat, his bare arms bearing his Golden Trophy Tower – he exults as The Conqueror, drinks in the adulation of the adolescent sea around him; he is startled by the sky-borne vroom of the upwards-sweeping Dream Cars, his beaming face swiftly mirroring, in the moment of his triumph, a greater wonder, a greater goal.

As funds for **Kustom Kar Kommandos** failed to materialize, Anger began to turn his attentions towards the burgeoning Haight-Ashbery scene in San Francisco, and the formulation of a new project: **Lucifer Rising**. (Anger was now living in Fulton Street, SF, in a mansion known as the "Russian Embassy".) Anger informed film critic Sheldon Renan that the film was to be his "first religious film", about a "holy" war between the Piscean Age (in decline) and the new, ascendent Age of Aquarius – epitomised by the conflict between kids and their parents, which was now escalating due to the advent of psychedelia. The casting of the film's protagonist produced some legendary tales. According to Anger, his first Lucifer was a 5-year-old boy named Godot, who killed himself trying to fly from a rooftop. He then met a "demonic" figure named Joe Lucifer, apparently summoned after Anger had performed Crowley's "Invocation of the Bornless One" in Golden Gate Park; this Lucifer disappeared after a few days, possibly returning to the insane asylum he had absconded from. Anger's next Lucifer was a certain Robert K. "Cupid" Beausoleil.[1]

LUCIFER RISING (A LOVE VISION) (1966)
1600 feet. Color. Filmed in San Francisco.
Cast: Bobby Beausoleil (Lucifer). No other details available. Edited footage stolen in 1967.

"It's a film about the Love Generation, but seen in depth – like the Fourth Dimension. It's about love – the violence as well as the tenderness... There's an invisible war going on... a war between the forces of life and death, love and hate.... I see the embodiment of love among the children as winning. Lucifer is actually a sunshine child..." –Anger, quoted in "Anger Rising"

Anger very publicly blamed the theft of *Lucifer* on Bobby Beausoleil, yet Beausoleil has always denied this, counter-claiming that Anger was in fact financially unable to reclaim his film from the processors; furthermore, he has suggested that the "theft" was in fact the first stage in an outrageous publicity stunt by Anger, the next part of which involved the filmmaker journeying to New York where, at the offices of Jonas Mekas, he reputedly immolated reels of unreleased, irreplaceable film. At the same time he publicly renounced film-making, placing the following full-page, black-bordered artistic epitaph[2] in *The Village Voice*: *"In Memoriam Kenneth Anger Film Maker (1947–67)"*.

The next stage of Anger's trip took him to Washington D.C., where he joined in a massive anti-Vietnam protest march on the Pentagon in late October (the filmmaker had already criticized the Vietnam War, describing it as "the establishment's way of masturbating young boys' violence" in an interview published in the *Los Angeles Free Press* the previous year).[3] Kenneth Anger next surfaced in London in 1968, where he entered into his dalliance with Mick Jagger[4] and commenced plans to edit the cutting-room fragments of the 1966 **Lucifer Rising** together with new footage to construct **Invocation Of My Demon Brother**, before starting the brand new version of **Lucifer** which would prove to be his final major film.

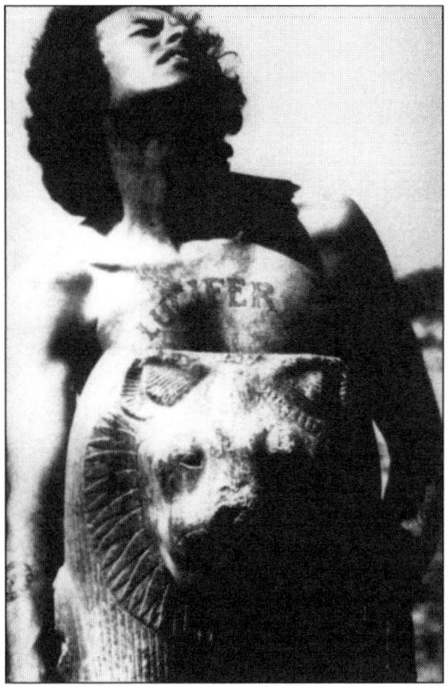

1. Beausoleil derived the nickname "Cupid" from a character he played in the 1966 movie **Mondo Hollywood**. His other movie roles included a part in the porno Western **Ramrodder** (1967), shot on the Spahn Ranch where he met another future mentor – Charles Manson.

2. Anger himself has described the "epitaph" episode as a "public exorcism" of his outrage and grief at losing **Lucifer Rising** (quoted in Rebekah Wood, "Flames In The Night").

3. In *The Family* (1971), Ed Sanders reports Anger's presence in Washington as follows: "While various Diggers and exorcists were standing atop the flat-bed truck screeching 'Out Demons Out', Anger, bare from the waist up, revealing what appeared to be a tattoo of Lucifer upon his chest, burned a picture of the Devil within a consecrated pentagram, shouting oaths and hissing as he flashed a magic ring at inquiring reporters thrusting microphones at him hunched down in the gravel" (p.43).

4. For a while, Anger had hopes that Mick Jagger – who wrote the moog synthesiser score for **Invocation Of My Demon Brother** shortly after the filiming of Donald Cammell's **Performance** in 1968 – would be his new Lucifer. "...The Magus instructed Jagger as to what rare occult books to purchase at London's more exclusive antiquaries. It was during the time that Anger served as the Rolling Stones' court wizard that Jagger read the 1930s novel *The Master And Margherita* by Mikhail Bulgakov, which tells the tale of Satan's visit to Russia after the revolution. The novel, and Anger's positive conception of Lucifer, inspired Jagger to write that enduring infernal anthem `Sympathy For The Devil'..." –Nikolas Schreck, *The Satanic Screen*, Creation Books 1999, p.132.

hijikata and the film image: corporeal revolt

Alongside Tatsumi Hijikata's work with photographers during the first years of his Ankoku Butoh project, he also undertook several collaborations with young experimental film-makers. In each case, the films were made rapidly, over two days at most, but they generated original works that used the medium of film to accentuate, confront or even oppose Hijikata's body and its gestures; those works did not attempt the kind of linear filmic documentation of his performances which Hijikata distrusted. In effect, those films form anti-documents of Ankoku Butoh, all the more revelatory and evocative for their tension and fragmentation in face of the body. It was through those film collaborations that Hijikata was able, to some degree, to resolve the dilemma of representation which obsessed all of Tokyo's experimental artists during that period: they desired a medium which would catch and project their obsessions in mid-gesture, or mid-act, with their charge of destruction or cruelty intact, but which would not engulf or defuse those gestures and acts into banality. Film caught Ankoku Butoh with the greatest immediacy of any medium, though the works which resulted were rarely seen in Hijikata's lifetime or in the subsequent two decades; the celluloid film prints in which the films existed were shown only at occasional events, at the Asbestos Hall itself (where Hijikata would dance holding the film projector in his arms, as he projected them) or in Tokyo's experimental cinema venues, and rarely outside Japan; it was the DVD medium, from the mid-2000s, that began to allow those films a wider audience. But exposure to those films proved essential for the choreographers and artists who were too young to have seen Hijikata perform himself, after his withdrawal into seclusion in the early 1970s; the engagement with Ankoku Butoh of internationally-renowned choreographers and performance artists, in contemporary Japan, such as Kim Itoh and Shinjin Shimizu (director of the 'Gekidan Kaitaisha' performance group), emerged primarily or solely from their awareness of it through the medium of film images. That preoccupation with the visual image, meshed conflictually with the human body, in the films of Hijikata's work, provoked a compelling creative strategy and source-material for many performance and digital-media artists in Tokyo, where the digital image had escalated to the status of an all-powerful entity in the decades after Hijikata's death.

Three experimental film-makers worked on collaborative projects with Hijikata from 1959 until the mid-1960s. Eikoh Hosoe, known primarily for his photography, made his sole film, **Navel And A-Bomb**, in 1960 (though he would also subsequently work as an assistant to Kon Ichikawa on that film-maker's documentary of the 1964 Tokyo Olympic Games), positioning Ankoku Butoh explicitly within the seared terrain of Japan's postwar history. The American film-maker and writer, Donald Richie, after being introduced to Hijikata by Mishima at the first performance of *Kinjiki* in May 1959, began collaborating with him almost immediately, on the film **Sacrifice**, and would make a further film with Hijikata, **War Games**, in 1962; those works formed part of a sustained body of experimental films which Richie had begun making as a teenager, while still in the USA, and which he continued to work on until 1968, with his final (and most notorious) experimental film, **Cybele**, before focusing principally on his writing activities. The young film-maker Takahiko Iimura was still in his twenties when he shot his two film collaborations with Hijikata, **Masseurs** and **Rose-Coloured Dance**, in 1963 and 1965; by that time, Iimura had already made a 'proto-ecological' film about the pollution and debris on the shores of

Tokyo Bay, **Junk**, and a film of sex acts, **Ai,** filmed at such extreme proximity that the sexual organs and gasping mouths of the participating figures became indistinguishably scrambled. Yoko Ono provided a soundtrack of cacophony for **Ai**, and like Ono, Iimura would abandon Japan and work principally in New York in the subsequent decades. He explored an experimental film language, derived from ideas on perception by the philosopher Jacques Derrida, around the material substance of the film-making process itself; in 2010, Iimura was still active as a film-maker and digital artist, working principally on CD-Rom projects. All three film-makers remembered their collaborations with Hijikata as seminal moments in their work.

Hosoe shot the twenty-minute film **Navel And A-Bomb** on a beach at Cape Taitozaki, near the town of Ohara, on a peninsula to the south-east of Tokyo, during the same, intensive period of collaboration in which he was photographing the gestures of Hijikata and the Asbestos Hall dancers in peripheral urban locations of Tokyo, and also photographing fragments of the stilled bodies of Hijikata and Akiko Motofuji for his *Man and Woman* project. The deserted marine landscape of Cape Taitozaki possessed a particular atmosphere for Hosoe: he perceived it as a resonant site, where compulsions that had been forgotten or hidden-away in an urban environment could still be unleashed. Hosoe became preoccupied at the time with the series of darkly-printed, Surrealism-inspired photographs which Bill Brandt had taken of beaches on the southern coast of England, though that preoccupation would prove unsettling; Hosoe, still only in his late twenties, felt that Brandt's photographs far surpassed his own beach-sited projects, and he abandoned them. **Navel And A-Bomb**, as a surviving element of those projects, makes direct connections between the body of Hijikata and the force of destruction which Hosoe perceived as being profoundly embedded in Japan, in its identities both as a mythologically-derived entity and as a post-atomic, consumerism-engulfed country. In the film, Hijikata (who supplied the film's obsession with the human navel) emerges from the sea as a capricious god of wrath, who steals away the navel of a child, thereby engendering a power of dis-equilibrium and chaos. Although the film possesses a dark core in its mediation of Ankoku Butoh, Hosoe's sense of exuberance, in making what he then hoped would be the first of numerous films, carries into the chaotic mixing of sensations which the film emanates; its sequences shift abruptly from humour to calamity and back again, and its soundtrack oscillates from that of lively jazz to the noise of a nuclear explosion.

Whereas Hosoe brought his knowledge of photographic composition to his collaboration with Hijikata, Donald Richie brought his own knowledge of the history of experimental film, especially that of France and the USA. In **Sacrifice**, Richie caught Hijikata and the Asbestos Hall dancers (including Akiko Motofuji) in a raw state of development, Hijikata's own movements still carrying the excoriating, violent gestures that had propelled *Kinjiki*, a few months earlier. Richie shot his ten-minute film on 8mm stock; only one print was made from the negative, and as though in empathy with Hijikata's 'dance of darkness', the film laboratory mistakenly printed it too darkly, so that the bodies' gestures in the film are half-submerged in obscurity. For the location of the film, Richie chose a deserted schoolyard, in an industrial zone of Tokyo's dockside Shinagawa district, and used music from Handel's *The Messiah* as his soundtrack. The film explored the shared preoccupation of Richie and Hijikata with rituals of death and resuscitation; after a celebratory procession of the dancers around the yard, one male dancer is segregated-off, then surrounded by the other participants who appear to urinate on him, defecate on him, and finally tear his chest open. Richie's concern was to create a visual alliance in film between sex and death, and his own inspiration in the film's style was taken in part from the French poet Jean Cocteau's films (Richie saw all of his own experimental films as 'poems' that demanded concentration from their viewers), and from an early film of 1947 by the American film-maker Kenneth Anger, **Fireworks**, which carries the same

preoccupation with the act of looking through the torn surfaces of the body, via the incising forces of desire and violence. At the *Kinjiki* performance that he had attended that year, Richie had grasped the volatile homoerotic charge of Hijikata's work, and he emphasized it in his film, meshing it with the aura of magisterial sexuality that Cocteau's film carried; Richie also wanted to accentuate the capacity he saw in Hijikata's Ankoku Butoh for anatomical transformation – the compulsion to move, almost without transition, from one sex to another, from life to death, and from youth to old age and back again.

Three years later, in the late summer of 1962, Hijikata and Richie collaborated on another film, **War Games**, which was shot over two days, this time on 16mm film stock, near the fishing village of Osato, on Kujukurihama, an immense, empty stretch of beach to the north-east of Tokyo, where they stayed together at a village inn. In some ways, **War Games** resonates with Hosoe's film (again, Hijikata would introduce a preoccupation with the human navel), though it carries far greater savagery and consistency. A typhoon tore across the beach during the filming, and long shots of the darkened storm-clouds and great waves punctuate the film. Although Hijikata's body doesn't appear in **War Games**, his presence and obsessions saturate the film; he and Richie were still preoccupied with rituals of death and resurgence, but this time, they focused those preoccupations on the figures of children, and on the memory and oblivion of conflict. Hijikata rapidly gathered together a gang of fourteen village boys, each of around ten years of age and wearing only swimming-trunks, attracting them with a handful of sweets. Richie filmed them in the act of caressing, then killing a goat on the beach, and solemnly burying it under a mound of sand, before convulsing with laughter and running away. He interposed shots of the tightly-grouped boys with shots of the facial planes of individual boys. The collective movements and facial gestures of the boys were choreographed with extreme discipline by Hijikata. Richie recalled that 'Hijikata was wonderful: he kept the boys in line, and kept them amused'. Richie wanted his film to seize the exact moment at which the boys become oblivious to the act of killing, and return to the rhythm of their everyday lives. In order to make that sense of oblivion emerge from the boys' faces, Hijikata began to perform a wild dance just outside the camera's range, pointing to his navel and then at the navels of the boys, whose facial expressions in the film transform from somber confusion to outraged hilarity and laughter. Richie remembered: 'Among the difficulties was the scene I wanted where the children, wide-eyed with knowledge of death, gradually forget what they have seen. They start to laugh, to play again, to go back to being children having fun on a beach... Soon all the little boys were laughing and pointing at each other, mouths open, eyes half-shut in mirth, and Hijikata still just outside camera range was dancing about, shorts slipping, the spirit of the festival, his navel like a large, comic eye. In the film, the children begin to laugh and their laughter is infectious. They point at each other, soon laughing so hard that they seem frantic with joy, so strong is their relief at being delivered from death.' (Donald Richie, 'Tatsumi Hijikata', in *Public People, Private People.*) As in **Sacrifice**, one figure is painstakingly segregated from the others, and when the gang of boys races away down the beach, the isolated boy remains with the goat, as the mound covering it is eroded by the typhoon and the goat's now-rigid body and mouth are revealed through fissures in the sand. Richie had shot his film without sound, and later assembled an intricate soundtrack of relentless typhoon roars, broken by bursts of ceremonial music which he had composed himself. Both of the collaborations between Richie and Hijikata explore processes of conflict: their impact on the human body, and also the amalgam of memory and oblivion within which they exist. And both films' action pivots on an interrogation of the responses open to the inhabitants of Japan (and of the wider world) at that moment of renewed conflict and dissent: submission, or resistance.

In his two collaborations with Hijikata, **Masseurs** and **Rose-Coloured Dance**, Takahiko Iimura was concerned with exploring an abrasive tension between the gestural act of performance and the film image. His films are very distinct from those which Hijikata made in collaboration with Hosoe and Richie; Iimura was not a friend of Hijikata, as those other two men were. When he asked Hijikata for permission to film his performances, Hijikata simply said 'okay' in a disinterested way. Iimura was already seen by his contemporaries in Tokyo as a 'difficult' film-maker – an impression that the subsequent four decades would not dissolve. In both films, Iimura's own figure invaded the space in which Hijikata's Ankoku Butoh was being performed, and his films appear, at first sight, to fall more into the genre of performance documentation than that of original film works. But the films are not documents; like the Austrian experimental film-maker Kurt Kren, who was filming the performance work of the notorious Vienna Action Group artists during the same years, Iimura was concerned to fragment and disrupt the illusion of documentation, and, instead, to probe the volatile zones of space and time between the film image and the human body. The films reflect Iimura's preoccupation of the time with the capacity of the film image to develop particular resonances of its own that emerged from its collision with the human body in movement. Hijikata's only role in those collaborations was to allow that exposure of his body, in the act of performance. Iimura moved rapidly between Hijikata and his dancers in the performance space, making provocative incursions, shooting at different angles and at different levels of proximity, and manoeuvring his camera into movements that existed in disjunction with those of Hijikata's Ankoku Butoh; Iimura called those films 'cine-dances'. The camerawork in the films which Chiako Nagano shot of Kazuo Ohno's outdoor dances, several years later, possessed a similar sense of movement in flux; however, Iimura's films were concentrated in the space and time of live performance in an audience-filled venue, and worked as an unsettling element in that performance. During the period in which Iimura's two films were made, between 1963 and 1965, Hijikata's work was seen in Tokyo as being essential to the culture of intensive cross-media experimentation ongoing in the city, between musicians, performers, poets, and visual artists of all kinds. However, Iimura's films focused on the way in which the presence of other media could be negated in the act of film-making, in order to accentuate the overriding impact of film; the footage Iimura shot was assembled into a rapid montage of blurred bodies and movements, as though the corporeal had been sieved-down to a ghostly, near-erased presence. The film image also bore traces of damage (scratches, incisions) over the image of the human body. Iimura's films experiment with their status as an autonomous visual counterpart to Hijikata's work. They probe the way in which human perception – that of the participant, and that of the spectator – registers performance actions, and the impacts which those actions hold: some actions are seized in their entirety, and others are only partially or peripherally captured. In many cases, by a contradiction that finally allied Iimura and Hijikata in collaboration, it was the incoherently perceived fragment of a live gesture that created a more evocative, direct impact on perception, rather than a smoothly assimilated, whole movement.

Towards the end of the 1960s – after the collaborations with experimental film-makers that had seized an imagery of Ankoku Butoh in its early stages were already over – Hijikata began to make occasional appearances as an actor in the commercial Japanese cinema, especially in extreme horror films of the 'erotic grotesque' (*ero guro*) genre; he continued to do so until his withdrawal into the Asbestos Hall in 1973. Those acting appearances were, for the most part, undertaken unwillingly, to make money, since Hijikata often had to rent the costly venues for his spectacles himself; and because those spectacles were only intermittently performed, for relatively small audiences, they generated too little income for him to survive and run the Asbestos Hall. But, since Hijikata made no compromise whatsoever in any field of activity he entered, and possessed limited capacity to adapt his habitual behaviour for the demands of the cinema, those film appearances profoundly resonate with his Ankoku Butoh preoccupations. Notably, he worked for the notorious director Teruo Ishii – and alongside the iconic swordswoman actress Meiko Kaji – on the film **Blind Woman's Curse**, made for the Nikkatsu studio in 1970, in the role of a maleficent hunchback named Tsuyoshi who serves as a henchman to a blind swordswoman now planning revenge on the clan whose young leader, played by Meiko Kaji, accidentally blinded her five years earlier. Hijikata's wild-haired hunchback, who communicates in delirious hisses and wild laughter, inhabits the subterranea of a freakshow theatre; he skins the snake-tattoos from the backs of the women of the enemy clan and licks the blood from the detached skin, in his attempts to ingratiate himself with his blind mistress. Although he has the uncanny ability to leap backwards from ground-level onto the roofs of adjacent buildings, he is finally gratuitously stabbed to death by a gang-leader, while on a mission of delivering a severed head. Set in the Akita town of Kisakata, close to Hijikata's birthplace, **Blind Woman's Curse** allows Hijikata two short sequences deeply imbued with his Ankoku Butoh work; in the first sequence, in preparation for bathing the blind swordswoman, he performs a dance among hanging metal panels like those he had used for his *Revolt of the Body* performances of 1968, and finally, following his stabbing beside a canal, his eyes wide and arms outstretched, Hijikata performs his death as an intricate gestural paroxysm for several seconds, then inverts his head and stares directly into the camera lens.

Hijikata's collaboration of the previous year with Teruo Ishii, for the film **Horrors Of Malformed Men**, made for the Toei studio, forms the most illuminating of his scattered film appearances in the 'erotic grotesque' horror-genre, and constitutes essential documentation of Hijikata's Butoh, even within the constraints of a narrative, fictional film. As with **Blind Woman's Curse**, elements drawn both from Hijikata's *Revolt of the Body*

performance, and also from the choreographic projects he was creating at the time for his Asbestos Hall dancers, appear – in an appropriately mutated and fragmented form – in **Horrors Of Malformed Men**. In the film, Hijikata took the major role of the webbed-fingered, monstrous outcast, Saigoro Komoda; as well as acting in numerous scenes, spitting and growling his dialogue, he also performed several extended dance sequences – filmed in a wild marine landscape of crashing waves and jagged black rock – that were intended to project the acute insanity of his character, who owns an isolated island which he intends to transform into his 'ideal world', full of 'wonderful things'. Having lured hundreds of beautiful young women to his island from Tokyo and surgically warped them, with their body-parts manipulated or rawly transplanted onto those of animals, he sexually subjugates the women to the island's population of bucktoothed anomalies and hunchbacks, planning to engender human mutations and corporeal fragmentations on a vast scale, with the ultimate intention of creating an outlandish anti-community of 'stranger and more fabulous malformed men', who will finally negate and terminally erase the normal, social world. His long-lost son Hirosuke escapes from a mental asylum in Tokyo and joins him on the island, instigating scenes of an idyllic celebration-ritual performed by the Asbestos Hall dancers; but the island's excessive concoction of incest, deformity and insane torture rapidly propels forward an apocalyptic finale, and the son eventually kills himself in an act of self-detonation that sends his detached body-parts and decapitated head shooting into the sky, while Hijikata's own character dies in anguish, blood streaming from his mouth, still obsessed with his dreams and hallucinations of all-engulfing human deformity.

The young director Teruo Ishii, who worked fast, was then engaged in a series of exploitation films on the broad theme of sexual torture, known collectively as **The Joys Of Torture**, at a time of chaotic transition in the Japanese studio system, as it attempted to find original subject matters that would reverse the decline of its film audiences in the new era of television. However, **Horrors Of Malformed Men** stood apart from the other films in Ishii's series, belonging more closely to the lineage of horror films of human mutation that emanates from Tod Browning's seminal **Freaks** (1932), and also drew its narrative from the work of the Japanese horror-mystery writer Edogawa Ranpo – an acolyte, as his name indicates, of Edgar Allan Poe – who had published the stories *Ogre of the Secluded Isle* and *The Strange Tale of Panorama Island* (the main source for Ishii's scenario) in the late 1920s. In casting his film, Ishii had realised that the role of the island's creator demanded someone with extraordinary presence, and an all-consuming obsession with corporeal transformation. He remembered: 'I approached Tatsumi Hijikata for the role because, without him, I could not have made the film the way I wanted. Without him, it would have been just another normal film.' Hijikata was receptive to the opportunity to place his Ankoku Butoh gestures within a new and contrary context, beyond that of art, and commented: 'Being drawn to the erotic and grotesque is an essential part of human nature. Teruo Ishii is great in pursuing this path, undaunted by criticism'. The film, shot on the remote Noto peninsula, on the northern Japan Sea coastline, and at Toei's studios in Kyoto, was released on 31 October 1969. Most of the mainstream cinema audience who watched **Horrors Of Malformed Men** on its release in Japan knew nothing of the peripheral art form, Ankoku Butoh; but they still absorbed its insidious gestures, from Hijikata's body, covertly. The film outraged and baffled its audience in equal measure, and closed after only a few weeks; the Toei studio viewed the unprecedented imageries of **Horrors Of Malformed Men** with distaste, withdrew the film's prints, and kept it out of sight for almost four decades. In 2007, the film was finally released on DVD in the USA, and found an entirely new audience, of viewers who perceived it as the maximally deranged, intensive embodiment of Japanese erotic-grotesque cinema, and of viewers entranced, too, by the miraculous re-emergence of long-lost but vivid filmic traces of Hijikata's Ankoku Butoh.

The body oscillates between carrying a profound anatomical shock, and deliquescing into a mist of deteriorating celluloid, in performance films of Hijikata's work. Fragments of the body in film destabilise it from its axis, and the equilibrium of the images themselves often veers wildly, ineptly, in the film-makers' attempts to capture those gestural transits through space, against darkness. Filming against that darkness often presented insurmountable challenges for the unsophisticated 8mm cameras used to seize Hijikata's body in the act of performance, and that darkness bleeds around the edge of the corporeal figure, always threatening to immerse it and render the image into utter blackness. Since Hijikata was resistant to having his performances set into banality by being documented, whole, in the medium of film, the friends and amateur cameramen who shot fragments of his performances worked under a further restriction: that of making their images glance sharply at the body's surface, subject to that repulsion imposed upon them by Hijikata. And since the cameras used to film Hijikata's performances had manual focus levers, the film-makers constantly struggled with the imperative to keep the volatile flux of Hijikata's gestures from blurring into visual incoherence.

In that straitened, pressurised form, the film image became a sensitised medium for recording Hijikata's body in the act of performance. Like many artists of the 1960s, Hijikata believed that the human body was under threat from a multiplicity of sources: warfare, cultural uprooting, consumerist urban environments, and also from a gradual unravelling of essential obsessions or narratives of the human body in transformation or glorious abjection. The Japanese body had literally changed in shape during the postwar decades, with the radical alteration in diet that the American Occupation and manias for European-style foods had brought: children were growing larger and stronger, and the bow-legged, bent-over peasant body of Japan was becoming rarer. Hijikata's transformation of the body, however, operated in another dimension from those superficial changes. He worked for a body that emanated vast panoramas of death, each minuscule gesture of corporeal contortion able to project an entire, concertinaed history of the body, in its essential aberrance, resuscitation, fury, and revolt. That transformation of the body in dance formed an ultimately fragile project, whose form of evanescing anatomical traces intimately allied itself to film, especially experimental film, in an era when the visual moving image possessed none of the ostensible indestructibility which it would later attain, in the digital era. Film often possessed a wilful, obstinate movement towards disintegration in the 1960s (a movement especially pronounced in works by film-makers with intractably focused aims, such as Takahiko Iimura), and that movement in film accentuated Hijikata's own movement into corporeal disintegration and vanishing.

Ankoku Butoh's rapport with film was one of the most intensive of the encounters between performance and experimental cinema in the 1960s, but it was far from being the only one. Performance artists and choreographers worldwide formed alliances, with greater or lesser degrees of tension, during that period. The films of corporeal fragments which Kurt Kren made for the Vienna Action Group artists in Austria carry many of the same dynamics as those made by the experimental film-makers with whom Hijikata collaborated in the 1960s; however, those Austrian artists, unlike Hijikata, had initially wanted conventional, linear records to be made in film of their scandalous, illegal performances, and had come to blows with Kren when they first saw how he had violently disassembled their work, and its space and time, within the medium of film (for one project, **Mama And Papa**, in 1964, Kren used a thousand editing cuts in a three-minute film). The individual aims of the experimental film-makers with whom Hijikata collaborated on original works were disparate, unified only by their lack of commercial intention: Richie remembered making his films purely for himself and his friends; Hosoe made his film, **Navel And A-Bomb**, principally as a gesture of friendship towards Hijikata; and Iimura made his own collaborations with Hijikata as cool tests, to further an ongoing theoretical exploration into issues of subjectivity and perception. By contrast, the film-makers (more exactly, 'cameramen', since they often operated anonymously, and lacked the tenuous prestige of experimental 'author'-film-makers) who shot films of Hijikata's performances had different intentions or imperatives. Hijikata expected them simply to seize moments of his body's insurgence, without defusing it.

The traces of those films of Hijikata's performances often risked becoming lost or overlooked, since no attempt was made to catalogue or preserve them during his lifetime; the film-reels were haphazardly stored at the Asbestos Hall, or remained in the possession of the cameramen. Hijikata's final solo performance of 1968, *Revolt of the Body*, in which he was alone on stage for over two hours, would be filmed by two cameramen, using black-and-white 16mm stock, one film lasting for fourteen minutes, the other for two minutes. Both films were elliptical, ineptly-shot, with the edited sequences in disorder, existing at an oblique tangent in time to that of the performance itself. Hijikata's illuminated body in movement was often barely discernible against the darkness of the performance space. However, Hijikata treasured those films of *Revolt of the Body* precisely for their malformations, and they would be his favourite films of his own performances. Other films of Hijikata's performances vanished and their traces appeared lost forever. His final performance with his dancers, *A Summer Storm*, took place in 1973 at the Westside Auditorium of Kyoto University (one of Hijikata's rare journeys outside Tokyo). On that occasion, the two young students who had organized the event arranged for it to be filmed in its entirety (along with a film of *Story of Smallpox* made at Tokyo's Shinjuku Art Theatre in the previous year, this was to be the only complete film of one of Hijikata's performances, at the moment when they reached their very end); three cameramen with small 8mm cameras filmed the performance in colour, one close-up to the dancers' faces and bodies, the second from the middle of the auditorium, and the third from the back of the hall. As with the other performances, the images of Hijikata and his dancers were outlined against a deep, engulfing darkness. The films were then almost forgotten, rarely if ever projected to audiences, and deteriorated over the following three decades; they became ghost images of Hijikata's body. Then, in 2003, one of the performance's organizers decided to restore and edit the fragile celluloid images, and digitally transferred them into a DVD document; in order to mark that DVD's commercial release, the film images of Hijikata's body, performing its terminal gestures for an audience, thirty years earlier, were projected at night, outdoors, from the immense digital advertising screens at the summits of department-store towers, in the centre of the teeming Shibuya district of Tokyo (the usual advertising images had been suspended for that short period). At the time when the film had been made, in 1973, no digital image-screens at all had existed in Tokyo, and the city itself had mutated beyond recognition in the intervening decades. Hijikata's body, now held in that new form of the digital image, and projected on screens far larger than any cinema screen, was brought into a resuscitated confrontation with the urban arena of Tokyo and its spectators.

Once the body has been erased, or the gesture of Ankoku Butoh has flared through space and vanished, nothing remains, except a set of traces and memories. But those fragile fragments of the body, in one of the supreme contradictions of Ankoku Butoh, tenaciously persist, transform, and survive: growing in significance and inspiration, while the forms of the visual image relentlessly mutate, and as time itself transforms and expands, inflicting new wounds, upon the body and the city, which resonate with the memories of Hijikata's Ankoku Butoh.

The seminal 'lost' Tatsumi Hijikata film, believed irretrievably vanished as a memory of Hijikata's work until its rediscovery in 2011, was one shot for projection at the Osaka Expo world's fair of March-September 1970, using an experimental shooting and projection system, 'Astrorama'. The film was titled **The Birth**, and was created to be shown in the Midori-kan (Green Pavilion), constructed to display Japanese innovations in image-

projection and related technologies, within the city-sized grounds of the Expo, located at the peripheries of Osaka. The event, together with the Tokyo Olympic Games of 1964, was intended to demonstrate Japan's new ascendancy and its postwar rehabilitation, and attracted vast, dense crowds and international attention throughout its duration. World's fairs and 'Expo' events have possessed an intricate and sustained history as showcases for experimental projection technologies; most notably, for the 1893 Chicago World's Fair ('World's Columbian Exposition'), Eadweard Muybridge constructed the first-ever purpose-built hall for the projection of moving-image sequences to public audiences, the Zoopraxographical Hall, within which he projected his sequences with his self-designed Zoopraxiscope projector. As a result, the Osaka Expo 70 was an ideal context for the developers of Astrorama, Goto Inc, to show off their new projection technology, developed in the same lineage as IMAX and intended for large-format projections and audiences, within expansive spaces. The inclusion of many avant-garde artists as participants in Expo 70 formed an attempt to accentuate the event's aura of innovation; Hijikata's collaborator, Tadanori Yokoo, was closely involved in conceptualising the event, and it provided valuable income for experimental artists whose work (as with Hijikata's) otherwise generated virtually nothing.

The Birth was shot on the slopes of the volcanic Mount Atosanupuri ('naked mountain' in the area's original Ainu language, and also known as Mount Io) in north-eastern Hokkaido, in June 1969; the volcano, close to the caldera Lake Kussharo, remained active and constantly emitted sulphurous steam. Hijikata, still recovering from the corporeal ordeal of his *Revolt Of The Body* performances of the previous year, remained rigorously self-isolated from the team of twenty-one Astrorama technicians, including their supervising director, Tomohiro Akiyama; he stayed alone at an inn on the shore of Lake Kussharo and refused all food, appearing each evening for the week-long filming sessions, which were shot at night. Hijikata appears in only one sequence of the ten-minute colour Astrorama film, as a magician or shaman – wearing a robe and with the distinctive long hair and beard from his previous year's performances, as though the film had irresistibly manifested itself as a coda to *Revolt Of The Body* – who originates the world as part-miracle, part-malediction; at the end of the sequence, Hijikata wildly leaps at and over the Astrorama camera. The film's incoherent scenario had been written by the poet Shuntaro Tanikawa who had specially requested Hijikata's appearance as the 'monstrous and grotesque' figure present at the world's formative dance-conjuration; other sequences displayed primal natural landscapes, and fragments of cities, about to be destroyed. A further sequence, shot in Tokyo, showed

Hijikata's Asbestos Hall dancers, filmed from above, naked and apparently engaged in sexual acts, the images superimposed with images of hell from paintings by Bosch and others. The Astrorama camera used five lenses simultaneously to create sensorially engulfing, multi-dimensional sequences recorded on a special 70mm film stock whose exacting development process required it to be sent to specialist laboratories in Hollywood for processing.

The Astrorama film was projected, with an ambitious system simultaneously projecting five celluloid film-reels, onto the internal dome of the Midori-kan, across five screens, thereby generating a 360-degree, immersive environment for its audiences. Fifteen million people are estimated to have visited the Midori-kan during the six-month run of the Expo, though most were in the act of rapidly passing-through the pavilion, as part of tour-groups, rather than gathering specifically to watch **The Birth** as an audience. At the event's end – as with all such spectacular, ephemeral expo-megalopolises, including the 1893 Chicago fair with Muybridge's short-lived Zoopraxographical Hall – the extravagant pavilions were immediately abandoned and left to deteriorate into ruins, despite the vast expense entailed in constructing them. Several years later, the site was almost entirely razed and converted into a suburban 'commemorative' park for the citizens of Osaka, with Expo 70's emblematic 'Tower of the Sun' allowed to remain standing at its entrance. Astrorama, too complex and cumbersome for commercial exploitation, also became redundant, and the original celluloid film-cans containing **The Birth** were stored-away without being documented, and forgotten, until researchers from the Hijikata archive at Tokyo's Keio University re-discovered them, forty years later, in the Osaka storage-facilities of the Sanwa Midori-kai alliance of corporations whose previous incarnation had sponsored the Midori-kan pavilion. The film had been preserved, more through oblivious neglect than active conservation, as a trace of the defunct Astrorama technology, rather than as a film-documentational residue of Hijikata's performance work or a record of the Expo 70 event itself. Rediscovered and re-projected, that document possessed all of the aberrant experimentation of Hijikata's work at its most vital moment. Film-memory itself forms a transformation, for the eye, from disintegration and oblivion.

index of films

list of illustrations

89 **Un Chien Andalou** (Luis Buñuel, Salvador Dalí, 1929).
91 **He Viva Dada** (Jean-Michel Humeau, 1965).
92 Yukio Mishima.
94 **Yûkoku** (Yukio Mishima, 1966). the severed head of Mishima after ritual suicide, 1970.
95 **La Séparation Radica-Doodica** (Eugène-Louis Doyen, 1902).
96 Albert Speer's *Zeppelinhaupttribüne*, Nuremberg.
98 **Kustom Kar Kommandos** (Kenneth Anger, 1964/5).
100 **Puce Moment** (Kenneth Anger, 1949); **L'Histoire D'O** (Kenneth Anger, 1961).
104 Kenneth Anger with Lucifer tattoo; Anger's 1967 artistic epitaph; Mick Jagger and moog synthesizer in **Performance** (Donald Cammell, 1968).
107 **War Games** (Donald Richie, 1962).
110 Tatsumi Hijikata in **Kyôfu Kikei Ningen: Edogawa Rampo Zenshû** (Ishii Teruo, 1969).
114 Location shoot for **The Birth**, 1969.